YO-AQY-030

Critical Issues in Educational Leadership Series

Joseph Murphy, Series Editor

Balanced Leadership

HOW EFFECTIVE PRINCIPALS
MANAGE THEIR WORK

Sheryl Boris-Schacter and Sondra Langer

Teachers College, Columbia University
New York and London

Published by Teachers College Press, 1234 Amsterdam Avenue, New York, NY 10027

Library of Congress Cataloging-in-Publication Data

Boris-Schacter, Sheryl.
  Balanced leadership : how effective principals manage their work / Sheryl Boris-Schacter and Sondra Langer
    p.   cm. — (Critical issues in educational leadership series)
    Includes bibliographic references and index.
    ISBN 0-8077-4699-1 (cloth : alk. paper) — ISBN 0-8077-4698-3 (pbk. : alk. paper)
    1. School principals—United States—Attitudes. 2. School management and
  organization—United States. 3. Educational Leadership—United States.
  4. Educational Surveys—United States. I. Langer, Sondra. II. Title. III. Series.

LB2831.92 .B67   2006

06-040398

ISBN-13:   ISBN-10:
978-0-8077- 4698-1 (paper)   0-8077- 4698-3 (paper)
978-0-8077- 4699-8 (cloth)   0-8077- 4699-1 (cloth)

Printed on acid-free paper
Manufactured in the United States of America

13   12   11   10   09   08   07   06   8   7   6   5   4   3   2   1

Contents

Acknowledgments

It has become almost difficult to remember life before we started traveling with the progressively weighty load of notes, drafts, data, books, and articles about the principalship. These concrete signs of our collaborative work followed us in boxes when we went on leave to the Rockefeller Center for Research in Bellagio, Italy; on sabbatical to Sydney, Australia; to a teaching assignment in Portland, Oregon; and to a summer home on Cape Cod. Our long-term friendship has been defined for the last 7 years by those boxes and the conclusions we drew from their contents. Like all travelers, we are both saddened by the ending and warmed by the memory. We would like to thank those who helped us along the journey.

In addition to the unnamed participating principals, there were several people we would like to name who conducted and transcribed interviews, entered quantitative data, performed library searches, and negotiated initial entry into school districts. These colleagues did an outstanding job, and we are grateful for their contributions. They include Christine Price, Jennifer De Chiara, Dennis Sweeney, and Lisa Bjork. We would also like to acknowledge the encouragement we received from our colleagues at Lesley University and the time and funds we were given by the School of Education in the form of sabbaticals, leaves, and grants.

From Sheryl: My beloved Blake and Tess progressed from being children to being teenagers during this book project. I could easily draw some clever comparisons, but I won't. Instead, I will acknowledge that their experiences in schools, both in America and abroad, influenced my thinking about school leadership and always helped me keep what was important at the core. Similarly, my husband, Bill, never failed to surprise, support, ground, or love me. I could not have picked a better life partner.

Finally, from Sondra: My appreciation to my children, Andy and Ellen, to their spouses, Nan and Nissim, and to their children, Noah, Emily, Joshua, Tamar, and David, for their stories about good teaching and good leadership. And, of course, I shall always be grateful to my husband, Larry, for his gracious support, insightful suggestions, and enduring love.

Introduction

This book is about school principals and the surprises they encounter in their work. Among these surprises is that educational leadership differs significantly from what well-educated, well-prepared, and well-meaning professionals thought it would be. We learned this from the compilation and analysis of stories, anecdotes, and vignettes told to us by more than 200 principals from across the United States. The stories describe how principals successfully reconcile their expectations and hopes with the realities and disappointments they encounter in their work.

The book describes the flexibility and resilience of school principals who view themselves as instructional leaders but who spend most of their time soothing emotional wounds, attending extracurricular activities, completing paperwork, and fixing physical plants. These principals strive to keep pedagogy at the heart of their work in spite of increasing personal demands and mandates from the federal, state, community, and district levels.

We placed the principals' testimonies in the context of recent educational reform efforts that acknowledge their link to academic achievement but limit the principals' capacity to lead. Based on what the principals told us, this hindrance has led to a profession in despair, with little recourse but for principals to be extraordinarily resourceful and creative. It is no longer enough to be only a charismatic leader. Today's principals must be collaborative, team-building, instructionally focused negotiators who work hard to hold on to their values, their families, and their jobs.

THE PRINICPAL SHORTAGE: THE BIG PICTURE

In 1998, we began reading mounting evidence of a national shortage of qualified principals (Educational Research Service, 1998; Keller, 1998; Yerkes & Guaglianone, 1998). Policymakers and educational researchers were compiling laundry lists of reasons and statistical projections of need, but nobody was asking the principals why the shortage existed or how it could best be addressed. We wondered what American principals thought about the following issues:

- Why the principalship has become less attractive
- Why current principals are leaving their positions
- How those who persist manage their work
- Why America's schools lack capable and willing new principal candidates
- Whether the role can be rethought to improve recruitment and retention and better meet academic goals

In order to answer these questions, we sought out the thoughts and voices of American principals, a constituency conspicuously absent from the debate. From 1998 to 2004, we received completed surveys and conducted interviews with just over 200 principals from across the country. The principals came from urban, suburban, and rural districts. They were male, female, White, and people of color. The principals led elementary, middle, and high schools in 12 states. Some were novices in their first or second years in the role, and some were seasoned veterans with more than 20 years of practice. All agreed to be interviewed or to complete our survey. Some provided unsolicited newsletters and memos as evidence of how they communicated agendas to the parents, teachers, and students of their schools. These documents provided additional data for analysis and inclusion (see Appendix A for a complete discussion of the methodology).

We attended carefully to the ideas gleaned from the interviews, surveys, and documents. This data helped us interpret how principals addressed professional persistence, managed competing demands, achieved life balance, and imagined new models for the principalship.

Three Principal Tensions

What emerged from our analysis of the data were three recurring themes that ultimately drove the structure of the chapters. The themes are portrayed in the book as opposing pairs vying for the principals' limited time and attention because that was how the principals characterized them. Because of the implied balance within the pairs and the principals' sense of choosing one activity to the exclusion of the other, we began thinking of them as "principal tensions." These tensions are:

- Instruction and management
- Work and personal lives
- Societal/community expectations and individual priorities

For example, principals reported that when they wanted to go into classrooms, they had to complete paperwork. When they needed to stay at school, they missed dinner at home. When the community expected them to respond immediately, they wanted to gather data and carefully consider options.

The principals talked about the struggle they faced dividing their time among these competing areas of responsibility. When we examined how principals approached the challenges of balancing the tensions, we found that they did not talk about issuing mandates, barking orders, or claiming the authority of being at the top of an organizational chart. Instead, they described how they worked with individuals and groups around policies, time, events, and traditions to get their positions heard and their agenda shaped. The study principals felt that they were most persuasive and effective when they used strategies that we labeled as negotiation.

The Role of Negotiation in School Leadership

When we analyzed the principals' stories, we found that negotiation took many forms. The principals described ways in which they do the following:

- Fashion compromise
- Make concessions
- Manage time
- Cooperate with others
- Foster relationships
- Define work boundaries

We grew to understand that the principals used negotiation to cope with the inordinate demands of the position.

The centrality of negotiation to successful leadership is not surprising to those who have long understood the relationship among leadership, power, and compromise (Fisher & Ury, 1983; Pfeffer, 1992). When principals employed these collaborative negotiation strategies, they reported that they were better able to influence colleagues, identify priorities, and solve complex problems. It seemed to us that the give-and-take of negotiation made the principals better informed, more influential, and more likely to reach their intended goals.

This book compiles, organizes, and analyzes these ideas and presents them in five chapters framed by our concept of negotiated tensions. We assume that this presentation will ignite ideas for other principals and policymakers of how to cope effectively with the existing school leadership structure and to seriously ponder new leadership paradigms that could address the principal shortage. It became clear to us that we must push beyond the current policy approaches to implement models that both alter the expectations of the principal and provide flexibility in the role's interpretation.

ORGANIZATION OF THE BOOK

Each chapter begins with a principal portrait. These portraits are not meant to present ideals or provide unusually dramatic stories. Rather, each is an amalgam of experiences conveyed to us by two or three actual principals working in real American schools and representing similar tales told by many others, although the quotations are verbatim. These vignettes present the principals' work in context, and they underscore and explain the negotiated tensions discussed in the chapters.

Chapter 1 puts the principal's work in historical and cultural perspective so as to provide the context for the discussion to follow. Chapters 2, 3, and 4 analyze the obstacles mentioned in the opening principal portrait in relation to the tension described in that chapter, and then discuss how those might be addressed through effective coping strategies.

Chapter 5 suggests alternative principal models and how they could work in practice. The Conclusion recaps the significant findings from the study, including implications for changes in policy and practice stemming from the principals' informed sentiments.

Chapter 1 addresses the question of what makes the principal's job so hard. It describes the present state of the American principalship and how it evolved to this point. We then connect the shortage to the collision of workplace conditions, societal expectations, and the accountability movement. The chapter details the research we did for the book and examines the two perspectives—psychological and sociological— that comprise the theoretical frameworks guiding our analysis of the principals' words. We applied these frameworks to the principals' stories in order to understand how they manage their workload, determine their priorities, carve out personal time, and elicit meaning from a role that others characterize as "impossible."

Chapter 2 captures the conflict between the myth of instructional leadership and the reality of managerial tasks. Principals repeatedly reported the anguish they felt when their daily duties were primarily activities that were not instructional in nature and took place outside of the classroom environment. The disparity between what principals think they should be doing and how they are actually diverted to other more reactive activities presents a huge challenge to principal persistence.

Chapter 3 focuses on the tension between the personal and professional lives of the principal. Principals vividly described the myriad of challenges to their "having a life" outside of their professional relationships and obligations. In fact, principals suggested that the degree to which they were effective in this regard was a central predictor of their longevity in the role.

The pressures principals feel from constituency groups and from governmental mandates are illustrated in Chapter 4. These comprise expectations of the role as well as of the person, including sociocultural mores and stereotypes regarding who occupies the principal's office and how that individual performs his or her job. The chapter outlines how principals apply negotiation strategies to balance community needs with personal values.

Chapter 5 offers structures and models for rethinking the work of the principal so that it reflects contemporary demands and lifestyles. It uses the principals' testimonies regarding the lack of balance in their lives to apply remedies through organizational and cultural strategies. It suggests that we could be more responsive to the needs of our nation's principals if we were willing to think flexibly about what school leadership means and what it could look like.

The Conclusion summarizes the major findings of the book and suggests ways in which we could use the principals' ideas to address their work conditions and enhance their persistence. We have great confidence in these recommendations because the principal data was so consistent that it constitutes a mandate for substantial and widespread change.

STANDARDS OF PRACTICE THAT COULD RESHAPE THE PRINCIPALSHIP

We learned that because principals lacked a range of recognized options for juggling priorities, they had to "customize" their responses. This meant that the principals created structures and negotiated with constituencies on an ad hoc, school-by-school, community-by-community basis. It is clear that principals are exhausted by these individual efforts, and this exhaustion is contributing to the principal shortage. Our research indicates that the profession must respond by providing standards of practice that allow all principals to do the following:

- Focus their time on instructional leadership
- Have a meaningful personal life
- Enjoy appropriate support at the workplace and in the community
- Experiment with flexible models of school leadership

Some ideas for standards of practice that would aid in recruiting and retaining qualified school leaders are contained in the proposals presented here by a cross section of American principals. The policymakers, principals, superintendents, school board members, workplace scholars, politicians, and university professors who read this book would do well to consider the suggestions, even when they would lead to a substantial change in how we do business. The future of school-based leadership may depend on it.

All names are pseudonyms. Place names and other details have also been changed to protect anonymity.

CHAPTER 1

Understanding the Principal Shortage and Why Current Policies and Practices Have Been Inadequate

After 21 years as a coach and teacher at the high school, Alex Cunningham was appointed principal at one of two middle schools in his hometown in rural South Carolina. He has held this position for the past 4 years. Alex told us that he can "think about work while I mow the lawn." It's a good thing, because he thinks about work for an average of 10 hours a week beyond the 65 to 70 hours that he ordinarily puts in at school. This does not include when the town uses his building to stage some of the events for the annual Peach Festival, which draws a crowd of between 50,000 and 60,000.

Alex is married to an educator who works in the district office; they have two teenage sons. The local school board requires that he reside in town. He admits that this is somewhat "old-fashioned" and complicates his ability to set clear boundaries between his work and family. However, it also means that his children's soccer games are usually geographically close to his office, making it more possible for him to attend at least some of them after school. He applies a formula to this parental obligation: "If I miss one game, I try to balance it out by getting to the next one." Alex, like many of his colleagues, wishes that the tasks of the principalship were neatly divided between those having to do with facilities management and those having to do with instructional leadership and teacher professional development. He admits that if he were to allocate more of his time to working with staff evaluation issues, then he would, by definition, lose touch with some of the daily building operations. His personality is such that he would have a difficult time delegating and relinquishing control to others. He concedes that "part of this problem is my ego and part is my willingness to initiate change and take responsibility for making things happen."

Alex works very hard and feels that he has to put more focus on managing his work and home responsibilities: "I'm driven, but I know that I can't achieve everything all the time. When I need to go home, there always has to be work left behind on the desk. At some point, there are just diminishing returns." Although he was talking about the daily tasks of the principalship, Alex also expressed the opinion that the progressively increasing workload in general was jeopardizing the future of the profession: "The years of having principals serve a school for 35 years are over. The job is just too demanding."

UNDERSTANDING THE PRINCIPAL SHORTAGE

Many of the principals in our study shared Alex Cunningham's observation that the principalship has evolved into an almost impossible position. The typical principal now works 54 to 80 hours a week (Gilman & Lanman-Givens, 2001; Yerkes & Guaglianone, 1998), is held accountable for student achievement on high-stakes tests, is increasingly involved with legal cases, and lacks the job security enjoyed by most classroom teachers. Escalating school violence and mounting pressure regarding the quality of public schools have led to political demands for privatization, vouchers, and charter school options.

The principals in our study indicated that the accountability movement has resulted in mounds of paperwork that detract from time that could be spent in classrooms. The number of hours devoted to paperwork was surpassed only by the hours required for meetings. The principals grumbled that, after completing forms and sitting on task forces, little time remained for substantive attention to instructional leadership and reflective practice. To make matters worse, some principals reported taking so much work and worry home with them every day that it interfered with their having meaningful personal lives outside of school. Principals seem to be underappreciated by a public that expects them to look like and act like the principal of their childhood without regard for the ways in which the world, the workplace, and the American educational agenda have changed. These factors have caused the study principals to report a degree of frustration and discouragement that they claim spawns attrition of experienced colleagues and discourages younger educators from pursuing administrative roles.

The Waning Attraction of the Principalship

So many disenchanted principals are choosing early retirement that we cannot fill the vacancies quickly enough with qualified applicants (Boris-Schacter & Merrifield, 2000). Demographics account for only a small percentage of the openings compared with the waning attraction of the job, including the comment by many of the principals in our study that their salaries do not significantly outpace those of veteran teachers in their schools.

Remuneration aside, Goodson and Hargreaves (2003) argue that there is another way to understand the current despair among American principals. They explain that educational reform efforts have changed significantly since the 1960s and 1970s, the early teaching days of many contemporary principals. During those tumultuous times, schools were social justice driven. Today, few would disagree that social reform and the educational agenda are market-driven. The globalization of education has presented 21st-century principals with the formidable task of reconciling the social justice issues of their early teaching careers with the current accountability mandates.

The principals' working conditions have also been modified in response to the virtual flood of reform efforts. These include organizational restructuring; increased accountability; and curricular innovations and instructional strategies that have been legislated by local, state, and federal agencies. Although these innovations benefit many of the nation's children, they have also left the principals in our study bemoaning inordinate amounts of paperwork, ambiguous lines of authority, and constantly changing professional goals. As a result, principals report feeling "tossed around by the whims of reform, constantly changing priorities mid-course in response to others' dictates."

Changing Social Conditions

Hurley (2001) explains how three critical areas of responsibility—special education, Title IX, and school safety—have dramatically altered principals' work in the last 30 years:

> Since 1974, special education programming has become a large chapter of public school life. These programs serve approximately 10 percent of public school students, and their governing regulations require the principal's involvement in several processes, including the diagnosis and programming of exceptional students. Likewise, the establishment of girls' sports teams following the enactment of Title IX has doubled athletic programming in middle and high schools. And, finally, the explosion of school safety concerns in recent years has meant that principals must develop and enforce new sets of school security policies. (p. 1)

Special education laws and Title IX are indispensable social reforms. Regardless of the merit of these reforms, the additional workload associated with their implementation is often daunting and underfunded. More recent federal legislation continues the trend of sometimes losing the point by hindering the principal with excessive paperwork, insufficient funding, and unrealistic implementation guidelines. For example, the federally mandated No Child Left Behind Act of 2001 (NCLB) is aimed at improving educational conditions and achievement for children living in poverty, especially in urban centers. One provision in the act allows for children to transfer from failing schools to better-performing schools. This has, somewhat perversely, caused overcrowding in some of the more desirable New York City schools, thus jeopardizing their efficacy: "I literally do not have a free room," said a middle school principal. "This is so unfair to kids, parents, teachers, and the community. NCLB is a nightmare" (quoted in Winerip, 2003).

Principals would be the first to underscore the growing need for schools to acknowledge the social and academic problems associated with poverty. However, most say that the overwhelming societal issues related to poverty are unfairly dumped at the schoolhouse door. The schools are just one institution of the community. We have grown to realize that issues associated with poverty must be tackled using a multi-agency approach. Coping with the emotional burden of children's poverty without sufficient community-based resources is cited as one of the reasons there is a dearth of school leaders in our urban centers (Kozol, 1991, 2005; Roza, 2003).

These evolving social conditions have, no doubt, contributed to Alex Cunningham's feelings that the job is now unworkable, a common position among our respondents. Blackman and Fenwick (2000) concur that the expectations of the principal's work have grown exponentially more complex:

> Today, the school leader is expected simultaneously to be a servant-leader, an organizational and social architect, an educator, a moral agent, a child advocate and social worker, a community activist, and a crisis-negotiator— all while raising students' standardized test performance. (p. 46)

The national shortage of willing, qualified principal candidates and a record number of early retirements confirm Cunningham's claim that the "larger-than-life" career principal of yore is a relic from another era. The shifting nature of the role (see, for example, Bradley, 1992; Christensen, 1992; Gilman & Lanman-Givens, 2001; Hurley, 2001; Murphy & Seashore Louis, 1994), insufficient compensation, and increased accountability have led to a national shortage of appropriate candidates for the principalship (Boris-Schacter & Langer, 2000; Boris-Schacter & Merrifield, 2000; Education Writers Association, 2002; Educational Research Service, 1998; Esparo, 2000; Institute for Educational Leadership, 2000; Keller, 1998; Leithwood, Janzi, &

Fernandez, 1994; Roza, 2003; Steinberg, 2000; Yerkes & Guaglianone, 1998).

Efforts to Stem the Shortage

As news of the principal shortage became more widespread, reports were generated that offered policy solutions (see, for example, Educational Research Service, 2000; Esparo, 2000; Institute for Educational Leadership, 2000). Among the recommendations were ideas targeting compensation, community respect, intrastate portability, credential reciprocity, and recruitment of women and people of color. Moreover, educational leaders sought to increase the desirability of the principalship by transforming the university-based preparation, increasing the remuneration, and implementing mentorship models.

In spite of these efforts, the urgency suggested by the reports, and recent success in recruiting women and people of color (Blackman & Fenwick, 2000), filling principal vacancies has been a slow process. In fact, the aspirant pool continues to shrink at elementary, middle, and high school levels in 47% of urban districts, 45% of suburban districts, and 52% of rural communities (Educational Research Service, 1998). According to the U.S. Department of Labor, this pattern is expected to continue:

> The U.S. Department of Labor estimates that 40 percent of the country's 93,200 principals are nearing retirement and that the need for school administrators throughout 2005 will increase by 10 percent to 20 percent. (Blackman & Fenwick, 2000, p. 46)

We suspect that the reasons for this are that policies and practices contained in the reports have not been widely implemented and that the public has been reluctant to change its expectations of who the principal should be, the parameters of the role, and the organizational structure of schools.

Looking for Help Outside of Education

Some communities have resorted, in the last 30 years, to looking outside of educational ranks to fill leadership posts. The assumption was that lack of efficiency was the issue, a throwback to the era immediately after World War II (Callahan, 1962). This approach has worked in some instances, has backfired in many, and has not made a significant dent in the overall need for new leadership. Schools are organizationally different from businesses and require leaders to have overlapping, yet distinct, sets of skills. The principals in our sample are less interested in the managerial activities currently associated with the role than in other aspects of the work, such as a deep understanding of pedagogy and adult professional development. In fact, many of them, including Alex Cunningham, made it clear that they would willingly delegate the managerial aspects of their work to someone with a business background.

Leslie Fenwick agrees that we do not have to look outside of education for worthy principals. She argues that the problem is not a lack of qualified educators; it is that teachers are aware of the liabilities of the job:

> We may not even have to look outside of education. . . . Look at why teachers choose to stay in the classroom. In the classroom, you can make a difference. To move on or become a principal, they see this as a totally opposite proposition. It means moving from influencing lives to becoming an educrat. (quoted in Education Writers Association, 2002, p. 6)

Since so many teachers, even those who are licensed as principals (Cusick, 2003), are reluctant to leave the classroom for the office, we must think of ways of supporting them. One is to make it possible for principals to continue teaching, and another is to encourage every appropriate candidate in the profession to consider leadership roles. New efforts for recruitment among women and people of color are essential. Not only would we tap into an underutilized resource that could help reduce the shortage, but we would be more likely to cultivate a principal pool that would more closely reflect the current and future demographics of America's schools (Blackman & Fenwick, 2000).

Even with recruitment from outside of the profession and increased efforts to cultivate underrepresented but appropriate candidates from within the profession, it is unlikely that a significant change in the number of appropriate candidates will occur. We believe that reformers, politicians, and school board members have only tinkered around the edges of this issue and that their efforts have not altered the shortage trajectory.

REPOSITIONING THE PROFESSION

The principals with whom we spoke want the principalship to change dramatically (Boris-Schacter & Langer, 2000, 2002). There is evidence to suggest that what we are currently expecting principals to do is unreasonable and that the generation of educators willing to fill this expanding role is dwindling. If we can no longer count on a principal to lead a school for a career, then we need to transform the role so that it is fluid enough to sustain significant change through the tenure of several principals. Since change takes time (Evans, 1996; Sarason, 1982), we need to reposition the profession so that school leaders can stay long enough to transform teaching practice, inspire students, and meet academic standards. The shortage commands our attention because we have long assumed that an effective principal is central to school improvement and student achievement (Archer, 2004; Cotton, 2003; Education Writers Association, 2002; Educational Research Service, 2000; Hallinger & Heck, 1998; Johnson, 1996; Kannapel & Clements, 2005; Rosenholtz, 1985; Rutter, Maughan, Mortimore, & Ouston, 1979).

OUR RESPONSE TO THE SHORTAGE: A NATIONAL STUDY

If we are serious about addressing the national shortage, we must add to the report recommendations the remedies provided by the principals in our study. A national leadership problem called for a national study of America's principals. Therefore, we asked practicing principals from across the country for their ideas about what constituted meaningful changes in the principalship. We asked them what obstructed and what facilitated their work. We hoped that conducting such a study would provide the debate on the principal shortage with a fresh set of ideas and a renewed resolve from its most salient constituency. The 200 principals we interviewed and surveyed from every region of the country demonstrated agreement about what mattered. Their responses were consistent regarding what challenged their personal and professional effectiveness, how they coped with those challenges, and how those coping mechanisms translated into alternative principal models.

When we began this research in 1998, others were investigating the complexities of life-balance issues by studying women's and men's experiences separately (Friedan, 1997; Goodman & O'Brien, 2000; Levine & Pittinsky, 1997; Smulyan, 2000; Zuckerman, 1999). We were convinced that the time had come to study the broadest possible cross section of principals in order to make useful recommendations regarding the balance between work and personal lives. Therefore, we included both male and female principals in our sample, reasoning that including both genders did not preclude us from analyzing them separately.

The results of our research indicated that successful principals of both genders held similar ideas regarding their work. They expressed these ideas in terms of balances between competing demands on their time. Over the course of any given day, principals reported responding to the constantly changing relationship among places they had to be, people they had to support, and tasks they had to complete. They named the following competing concerns:

- Classroom and office
- Home and school
- Needs of teachers and needs of students
- Demands from the community and the principal's vision
- Instructional program and managerial responsibilities
- Central office and building-level priorities

In most instances, the principals viewed these opposites not as diametrically opposed demands on their time and expertise but as complementary components of their work lives. We wondered how they managed the complex balance necessary to fulfill the existing expectations of the principalship. Based on the evidence of principal tensions, we drew on theoretical frameworks from the fields of psychology and sociology for aid in making sense of the principals' stories.

A Psychological Framework: Adult Balance

Robert Kegan's (1982) research seemed useful to us in thinking about the perpetually changing priorities that characterize the principals' roles. He writes about the management of the relationship between seemingly opposite poles in his discussion of Gilligan and Murphy's work on post-adolescence. Kegan suggests that when adolescent idealism evolves into psychological maturity, "the orientation seems to shift to the relationship between poles in a paradox rather than a choice between the poles" (p. 229).

Kegan defines adult development in terms of balance, and he cautions that balance frequently brings with it the possibility of losing one's balance. He describes the adult "experience of defending and surrendering the balances we are, we have been, and we will be throughout the lifespan . . . each balance suggests how a person is composed, but each suggests, too, a new way for the person to lose her composure" (p. 114). The concept of adult balance that he finds so prevalent in the literature is not a phenomenon that we should attempt to eliminate. Instead, we ought to study the successful strategies people employ to manage the relationship between the two poles of activities demanding balance. It is this process of negotiation between and among poles that became the focus for this book.

It was reasonably easy to see how principals made decisions when one pole or the other presented a compelling need for immediate attention.

However, we became interested in knowing how principals managed the balance between competing poles when the need for attention by each was equally strong. We turned to Michael Lipsky's *Street-Level Bureaucracy* (1981) for assistance.

A Sociological Framework: Transitioning from the Classroom to the Office

Lipsky coined the term *street-level bureaucrats* to describe "public service workers who interact directly with citizens in the course of their jobs, and who have substantial discretion in the execution of their work" (p. 3). He names teachers, judges, social workers, and police officers as examples of street-level bureaucrats because they are "public employees who grant access to government programs and provide services within them" (p. 3). Lipsky argues that street-level bureaucrats apply personal definitions of quality work and acceptable levels of efficiency as a means of meeting the huge demands of a single workday. Principals in our study reported that increased workloads and increased accountability, coupled with decreased budgets, have complicated their ability to get their work done. Impossible workloads prevented these principals from feeling that they were successful in all aspects of their job.

Lipsky explains that managers are different from street-level bureaucrats in that they "are interested in achieving results consistent with agency objectives. Street-level bureaucrats are interested in processing work consistent with their own preferences" (p. 19). If we apply Lipsky's distinction regarding agency objectives and professional objectives, then school principals are neither street-level bureaucrats nor managers.

The ambiguities regarding which of the two categories better describes the principal provide an example of the problem of viewing the principal as a middle manager. Clearly, the level of autonomy and discretion is vital in both roles, but the dilemma of principal as middle manager is how to merge the agency's goals with those of the principal. Unlike the classroom teacher whose responsibilities lie primarily with her or his students, the principal is accountable to teachers, parents, central office administrators, and policymakers.

There are far fewer opportunities for principals than there are for teachers to concentrate on self-defined professional priorities. There is also greater pressure on principals to move toward compliance with agency policy than there is for teachers. Ironically, as the principal gains more positional power within the hierarchy of schools, his or her control over work life and personal life diminishes. The contrast between the life of a teacher as a street-level bureaucrat and the life of a principal as both a street-level bureaucrat and a manager illustrates the trials many principals face when they move from being a teacher to being an administrator. Most teachers negotiate with a single classroom of children and their parents; their professional goals are clear, and the parameters of their work are relatively defined. For the principal, the process of negotiating is more expansive because it involves a greater number of people within a context of heightened ambiguity. We wondered what this increased complexity meant for the principal today.

Applying the Theoretical Frameworks to the Principal Study

The theoretical frameworks offered by Kegan and Lipsky provided a way for us to think about the data and its analysis and to better appreciate the concept of balance in principal work. From that understanding, we identified three pairs of tensions common to all of our study respondents: instruction and management, work and personal lives, and societal/ community expectations and individual priorities. These are discussed in depth in Chapters 2, 3, and 4, respectively. In Chapter 5, several alternative principal models are described for professional consideration. Their construction was based on our analyses of the identified tensions and the ideas of the participating study principals.

CHAPTER 2

Negotiating Instructional Leadership and Managerial Tasks

Amanda Jackson was a classroom teacher and curriculum coordinator in a suburban elementary school for 12 years prior to becoming a principal. For the majority of that time, she had no desire to be a principal, but the longer she taught, the more she felt that the job could be right for her. Based on her years of effective teaching and supervision, she felt that she could provide better instructional and curricular leadership than was presently in place. In her mind, teaching and learning were at the heart of the enterprise, yet she observed her principal spending much of his time directing traffic, reminding children to clean up after themselves in the cafeteria, and completing endless paperwork. Amanda's principal rarely initiated substantive conversations with her or her colleagues around issues of professional practice. Amanda wondered whether the principalship had to be that way.

Amanda is now in her third year as principal. Her family resides in the Northeast in the town next to the one in which she works. She is married and has two children who were 9 and 12 at the time of her appointment. Her husband, a computer programmer, is extremely supportive of her career, works at home, and shares house-related responsibilities.

In addition to her desire to be a great principal, Amanda's decision to pursue the principalship was also fueled by the economy. Her husband's position in technology no longer looked as secure to them as it once had. Although the principalship meant working additional hours and having less job protection, it also meant a modest pay increase. Amanda and her husband, Donald, reasoned that, even if the principalship did not work out, the teacher shortage meant that she could likely resume her work in the classroom. After all, the continuous improvement of teaching and learning is why she became an educator.

Their children are now older and do not require full-time care. Nonetheless, Amanda is grateful that Donald's work allows him to maintain a watchful eye. This enables her to spend more time and energy on the daily requirements of the principalship. As part of her position as educational leader, she feels the need to be in the classroom as well as in the office. Although she knows that she can't be perfect at every aspect of her work, it doesn't stop her from feeling bad or even guilty about not doing what is required of her or what she considers to be essential. In fact, the tension she had observed her former principal display between management and instruction also plagued her. She said of herself, "I consider myself to be more of a mentor/master teacher than an administrator, but you can't always tell that from how I spend my time."

Regardless of how early she arrives at school, there are always people, messages, and e-mails waiting. When she walks down the halls, teachers, custodians, and parents always stop her. Amanda understands that a big piece of her work is to keep the school going. This often means being reactive instead of proactive. New instructional programs come into the school, and the need to spend concentrated time with students and teachers is hardly ever possible. Amanda does not feel that an intellectual activity such as learning new curricula should be relegated to a "part-time, fit-in-between-everything-else basis." Yet, she constantly struggles with this issue.

Amanda sees supervision and modeling instruction as the essence of her job but teacher evaluations and supervision are time consuming, and the write-ups are burdensome. She has tried to model lessons but rarely finds adequate time to do so. She visits classrooms for 5-minute "walk-throughs," but they are not completely satisfying to her or to the teachers. Providing useful feedback requires time for reflecting and building trusting relationships. Unlike principal colleagues she knows, Amanda feels strongly that this task cannot be delegated to others, but she also feels that the administrative details prevent her from being the instructional leader she envisioned. When she spends most days in the office writing reports, sending messages to staff, and answering phone calls and e-mails, the focus of her movement to the principalship is obscured. She wonders whether the small pay differential offsets the number of hours and degree of frustration.

DEFINING INSTRUCTIONAL LEADERSHIP

In the context of our research, we never directly asked principals to define *instructional leadership*. However, it became easy to extrapolate definitions from the coupling of the activities with the use of the term. Like Amanda, respondents talked about their role as one of mentoring staff, modeling instruction, visiting classrooms, and providing customized professional development experiences. A middle school principal wistfully listed these activities of instructional stewardship as those that would define her notion of "the dream principalship":

The dream principalship would be focused around teaching and learning. It would include maximum amount of time in classrooms, it would include minimal paperwork, it would include at least one period a day in which I could teach and model good instruction to other teachers in the building. The ideal principalship would involve enormous amounts of time mentoring staff people and developing professional development themes for the entire school.

This one principal's notion of a "dream principalship" turned out to be a common paradigm. It was also, for almost all of the principals in our study, a dream not realized.

OBSTACLES TO LEADERSHIP

Amanda Jackson's experience illuminates the principal's role as both manager and street-level bureaucrat. On the one hand, there are minute-to-minute demands on Amanda's time to oversee the daily operations of a school building and its occupants. On the other hand, she is less interested in some of those responsibilities and more invested in championing academic achievement. Even though she left the classroom to become an instructional leader, defining her "true" work in such narrow terms is leading to professional frustration and perceived failure. She is working toward reconciling the facts that she has gained positional power in her school but has lost much control over her work agenda.

This lack of control over one's work agenda can have a significant effect on relative happiness and harmony, maybe even more so than control over one's time. In an essay from the *Chronicle of Higher Education*, Ellen Ostrow (2003) explains that if one cannot control daily activities, then one has less control over the outcome of daily events. She suggests that this lack of control threatens a person's sense of balance. Given our argument that principal work is comprised of many kinds of negotiation within dynamic balances, this sense of agenda control is significant:

> Instead of a time-oriented approach, try to think about balance in terms of what you would need to happen for you to feel in harmony—i.e., for you to feel that you're at your peak, experiencing relatively more positive than negative emotion, feeling in control of your life, focused on meaningful goals of intrinsic importance. There may be considerable juggling going on, but from moment to moment, this is how balance feels. . . . Fundamentally, harmony and balance derive from a sense of personal control over our work and our lives. By personal control, I mean the sense that you can influence the outcome of significant events. Feeling like you can choose among outcomes

and cope with the consequences also defines personal control. (Ostrow, 2003, p. C5)

Less Control, More Authority: From the Classroom to the Office

As a classroom teacher, Amanda was able to devote the vast majority of her time to teaching and learning. The realization that this is not generally true for principals is a hard lesson felt in schoolhouses across America. In the transition from being a teacher who is a street-level bureaucrat to being a principal who is also a manager, the principal frequently surrenders discretion over his or her professional priorities. The tension between former tasks as street-level bureaucrats and new functions as principals is yet another balancing act that must be artfully negotiated. In our interviews and surveys, principals bemoaned that sometimes the new job hardly seemed worth the effort necessary to make the transition successful. As one principal observed, "A new principal doesn't necessarily make more money than an experienced teacher, works much longer hours, and doesn't get dental coverage or have job security. The principal doesn't even control her work. Who wants to deal with those hassles when you can have your own classroom?"

Principals Are Consumed by Noninstructional Activities

The study principals indicated that the disappointment they experience regarding the relatively small amount of time that they actually devote to instructional leadership is the most stunning obstacle they face to job persistence. Worse yet, what prevents them from devoting more time to instructional leadership is often activities that they view as unsuitable for the principal. For instance, they regretted their required attendance at "useless" meetings, their need to complete reams of paperwork associated with federal and state legislation, their community's preoccupation with real estate prices tied to standardized test scores, and the myriad constituency demands that principals regarded as tangential to the mission of teaching and learning. As a midwestern elementary principal bluntly put it, she is spending "more time pulling weeds than planting seeds."

A high school principal explained how his current position was challenging him professionally and physically because, unlike in a previous principalship, he did not have the benefit of a business manager to whom he could delegate noninstructional tasks:

> When I started this position, I had to give up playing golf. Consequently, my blood pressure shot up and I had to take some time off to get it back under control. Principals now have more responsibilities than we used to have: food service, budget, building maintenance. At my previous school I had a business manager. Every school should have one to take care of purchase orders, money transfers, etc. It used to be that the principal was primarily an instructional leader which is what I need time for now instead of going to ridiculous meetings to learn about paperwork.

Too Little Time for Instructional Leadership Threatens the Principal's Professional Identity

It seems that Amanda's struggle with finding adequate time to be an instructional leader in her building is no less than a struggle with professional identity and purpose. The balance is the cognitive dissonance between what principals imagined they would be doing before assuming the principalship and how they actually spend their time. This dissonance leads to a malaise for some principals. Others express it as resignation. Still others, like Amanda, are frustrated but determined. As one starry-eyed middle school principal lamented, "There is not nearly enough time to spend in classrooms and roaming the halls. I feel like I am in the business of compromise, not perfection, but I keep trying." Not surprisingly, we found that frustration leads principals in one of two directions: Either they learn to successfully negotiate the numerous balances inherent in the position, or they quit.

Even more than the other balances in the principalship, the balance between instructional leadership and managerial tasks raises the question, "What is the role of the school principal?" Historically, the principalship has been one of "head teacher," but the position has evolved into one of data analyst, public relations liaison, and accountability officer (Pappano, 2003). Like principals in other studies (Lovely, 2004), our principals wanted little to do with these managerial aspects of the new principalship and much more to do with pedagogy. Suzette Lovely (2004) described this change as "the 'benevolent dictators' of the past being replaced by the instructional maestros of the future" (p. 7). Although poetic, this characterization is not quite accurate. The "head teacher" was an instructional leader who led and mentored by example. In a back-to-the-future sentiment, the principals in our study seem to be longing for their role to include much more of what was originally intended by the creation of the school principal. Therefore, the "instructional maestros" are of the future and of the past. We would argue that the benevolent dictators were organizational aberrations that grew from the sociocultural stereotype of the paternal principal and have limited relevance to the contemporary principalship.

Outside Demands Distract Principals from Instruction

This balance between instructional leadership and managerial tasks was the issue causing the most concern among our study principals. They felt challenged by the need to align competing and externally driven demands with their personal definitions of effective leadership. When faced with the contrast between a teacher's life of direct service with children and a principal's preoccupation with mounds of paperwork and fire dousing, the principals had to convince themselves that their work was worthwhile and that their focus, if not the amount of time they spent, was always on instruction. This delusion seemed to justify the workload, the loneliness, and the time spent away from instructional leadership. Many of these principals employed this approach to balance the tension between instruction and management. We are convinced that this is a reasonable coping mechanism employed by dedicated professionals who wish the job were different.

For instance, Steve, a high school principal in an urban district, spoke for many of his colleagues when he characterized constituency demands as "distractions" from his primary focus of teaching and learning. However, he went further than many other principals by describing his role as one of "arrogant" guardian of his school's focus on instruction:

> I'm a little arrogant. I'm always reminding myself that I'm the best person for the job. When the powers that be are trying to define what measures teaching and learning, they don't always have a clear-cut idea. The challenge is having teaching and learning happen and being focused on this despite distractions from the central office, community, and parents.

One cannot help but conjure an image of a lone defender of the realm, standing between the well-meaning but misinformed interlopers and the students. A different urban principal viewed the central administration as being less benign, arguing that the interference was toxic to the learning environment and that the principal's role is unambiguous regarding his or her duty to run interference between the bureaucracy and the teachers:

> I can't imagine why being a principal now would have any appeal as a career. Despite the buzz that the principal is supposed to be an instructional leader as opposed to the person who buffers the people in the school from the horrible bureaucracy of the outside school department, the reality is that the outside school department, if left to its own devices, would make working in schools pretty well intolerable.

Managerial Tasks That Undermine Instructional Stewardship: Paperwork and Meetings

The degree to which the principals shunned managerial tasks such as paperwork and considered them an obstruction to the profession was notable. For instance, Bill, a veteran elementary principal, spoke for many principals in our study when he explained that doing paperwork prevents him from interacting with people and should not even be part of his work: "I like to focus on the kids and work with staff and parents around instruction—the people side. I guess it comes down to people versus paperwork. I like the people part, but I have to do it all. I would love to have someone else just do the paperwork for me so that I could just do my job."

Principals resented the time-consuming nature of paperwork because it limited their instructional leadership capacity. Amanda grumbled that fulfilling mandates from state departments of education and the federal government, frequently testing children, and writing reports to political constituencies required that she spend time and energy away from her role as instructional leader. An urban high school principal described the paperwork as being "unbelievable, as though the central office departments don't know what the others are doing. There are too many meetings; I am out of the building too much." Fran, a 5th-year middle school principal from a district in the western United States, underscored the degree to which central office paperwork is a major obstacle to a principal's effective use of time, time that could be spent as an instructional leader: "I am constantly thrown off balance by the central office providing five different and conflicting sets of directions for a single project."

One 1st-year principal we interviewed indicated that she wanted to "start off getting to know the people rather than the job." She explained that her concern was with interpersonal relations rather than with traditionally defined effective administrative activities that "often entailed paperwork." She reasoned that before she could delegate responsibilities to others or facilitate improved instruction, she needed to know her faculty's strengths and build their trust. Regardless of whether this approach proves doable in the long run, its articulation provides yet another example of how principals shun managerial tasks and blame them for drawing their attention away from instruction.

A different 1st-year principal was, perhaps, more realistic when he conceded that the principalship, as conceptualized, does not allow for concentrated time in instructional leadership. He implied that having wonderful teachers ensures the endurance of the enterprise but made clear that he is not professionally happy with the arrangement:

> You learn real fast that being a principal has very little to do
> with instructional leadership. That's such a tiny fraction of
> what I do right now. I would be so happy with my job if I could
> concentrate on instruction, but that's not going to happen for
> a while with a building project going on. You just have to trust
> that your good people are doing their jobs, and then concentrate
> on supporting the teachers who are marginal.

Even the more experienced practitioners felt that they did not focus sufficient time on instructional improvement. Instead of spending after-school hours planning professional development activities, developing schoolwide curricular themes, and reflecting on pedagogical practice, principals described this time as being filled with "catch-up." There was little mention of artistry, problem solving, or craft enhancement. Marsha, a midwestern principal, depicted the great care she took to prioritize and organize her managerial tasks, which, to her dismay, almost always came before instructional leadership:

> I work at home. I work on the weekend. I categorize things and
> organize them into folders so I have everything right where I
> need it. I don't have the time to look for things. I answer e-mails
> and phone calls right away. I take care of students first, then
> teachers, then I pay attention to the organizational management
> duties of the principal. There's hardly ever time for anything
> else, like instruction.

A different principal said she was forced to do paperwork after the schoolday was over as well as after family members were asleep: "Written work I don't finish after the kids leave, I bring home. I resume my work after 9:30 when the children go to bed, and I work for 2 or 3 hours. My husband teases me that I must not have enough to do if I turn off the bedroom light before 11:00 or 11:30."

Paperwork That Supports Instruction: Observation Write-Ups and Professional Development Plans

There are two related kinds of paperwork that principals felt furthered their role as instructional leaders: observation write-ups and professional development plans. If improving teaching and learning is the heart of the enterprise, then the principals in our study view teacher supervision as the central task of their work. This identification makes it extremely difficult to delegate to others without jeopardizing the principal's sense of efficacy. Based on what principals said and how many of them said it, we do not think we are overstating the case.

Unlike the reactive tasks and split-second decision making that characterize the majority of the principal's day, staff evaluation requires reflection, structure, and "long blocks of quiet time." Since long stretches of uninterrupted time are rare in most schools, teacher evaluation write-ups are, more often than not, designated as homework. Principals did make the distinction between the supervision of teachers with professional status and those who were less experienced, with newer teachers requiring more administrative feedback. This means that, for the foreseeable future, the principals' evaluation workloads will increase as more and more young recruits and career-changers join the teaching ranks.

Most principals did not complain about the additional hours it took to coach neophytes, observe their work, meet with them, and fashion professional development plans. However, principals did say that supervising poorly performing teachers, be they new or veteran, took an emotional toll and had a tremendous effect on their workload. An East Coast principal described the discrepant workload between evaluating strong teachers and evaluating teachers in need of improvement: "A good evaluation takes me 1 hour to write up; I know because I timed it. A bad evaluation takes between 2 and 3 hours, and has to be carefully worded, two to three pages long, and airtight. It's draining."

We wondered how these drained principals, inundated with paperwork and other managerial tasks, coped with the pressures and perceived assaults on their professional identity as instructional leaders.

EFFECTIVE COPING STRATEGIES

If the tension is between instructional leadership and managerial tasks, how do principals successfully negotiate that tension? If educators move into the principalship in order to fulfill the role of instructional leader, then how do they organize the overwhelming time demand of activities such as building maintenance, district meetings, supply ordering, schedule construction, legislative compliance, and budget matters so that there is room for instructional stewardship? As we already explained, the partial answer is that most principals learn quickly that the current job conceptualization includes little structured time for proactive, thoughtful reflection on pedagogy. Therefore, persisting principals shift their expectations and create customized responses that suit their individual personalities and work styles.

As was true for each of the tensions of the principalship, we found that the principals in our study effectively coped through artful negotiation. In this instance, their responses fell into three categories:

- They successfully negotiated with central office personnel to participate in hiring building-level staff.
- They successfully negotiated the delegation of tasks to others.
- They successfully negotiated their schedules so that there was deliberately structured time for designated instructionally related activities.

Hiring the Right People: Creating Compatibility and a Shared Instructional Agenda

In addition to defining instructional leadership as mentoring, supervising, and evaluating staff; visiting and teaching classes; shielding the school from outside interruptions; and arranging professional development opportunities, the principals in our study mentioned talent brokering as another way in which they contribute to the mission of the public schools.

Like other professionals, principals feel that one of the most important ways in which they safeguard the integrity of teaching and cope with the pressures of the position is through hiring. We found that the extent to which principals are able to select their staff is a strong predictor of principal longevity. This was no surprise.

Typically, the principals described their role in hiring quality school personnel as being "vital to the academic success of children." One elementary principal from the South explained that hiring the right person into the right job is central to his being an instructional leader and effectively managing his time:

> Principals are talent brokers. We need to have great teachers in the right positions. We have to go into classrooms and assess instruction, and that assessment process is grueling and time consuming. It is incredibly helpful if we hire the right person in the first place.

Until very recently, when veteran teachers began retiring and the children and grandchildren of baby boomers began attending school, few teaching positions had been available for several years. When openings occurred, principals were not empowered to conduct independent searches. It is much more common for these decisions to be made at the central office level, even under school-based management and even when it is the principals who are being held accountable for building-level academic achievement. It is also true that principals are usually prevented from dismissing underperforming school-level personnel. This is the quintessential middle-management dilemma of having responsibility without adequate authority. When principals were successful in breaking through this dilemma, the challenge of time management was addressed.

For instance, David, a middle school principal for 18 years, explained that he is inefficient and has to work long hours because of it. He noticed, however, that lately his work habits have been different. His time management skills have improved dramatically as a result of his finally replacing a poor secretary: "This year, I hired a secretary who could easily run the place. She wants to leave every day by 3:00, so all the work has to get done before then. It's been a bit overwhelming to change the pace after 17 years, but I finally feel that I have an ally."

A different middle school principal, Jack, underscored the need for "bringing in the right people." He explained that his influence as a principal of a large 850-student school is primarily through his having hired approximately "75% of the staff over [his] 14-year tenure." This principal has built an infrastructure of handpicked department chairs who carry out his instructional agenda by providing direct teacher supervision to the majority of the staff. The principal supervises only the new teachers and the ones in need of extra support.

Given that staff supervision is the most time-consuming task named by the principals in the study, it was little wonder that Jack "rarely took work home with [him] anymore." There was a developmental component for most principals in our sample regarding working at home, with those who are newer logging in many, many more at-home hours. There was also a direct correlation between a compatible staff and a principal's workload. Jack had both years in the role and multiple opportunities for hiring, a pairing that often goes together. Principals new to the position or to a school must create other ways of efficiently affecting whole-school instruction while waiting for hiring opportunities.

Creating a Climate That Encourages Experimentation

In the absence of hiring teachers, principals told us that they exert instructional leadership by controlling the professional development agenda and by creating a school climate that encourages pedagogical risk taking. Even if a schoolwide cultural transformation fails to get every teacher to try different approaches, principals concede that the effort is worthwhile if at least some teachers experiment with content, delivery, or assessment strategies.

Matt, a middle school principal in the Northeast, explains his efforts in creating a school culture of professional daring: "In addition to offering professional development opportunities that force teachers to explore different content areas from their own, I explicitly encourage people to take risks. I allow people to make mistakes, something we feel less free to do in this age of accountability . . . we fall into a trap of maintaining the status quo. We need to model professional courage."

Sometimes modeling professional courage involves delegation of tasks. The literature of organizational theory has long recognized the power inherent in the giving away of power (see, for example, Bolman & Deal, 1997; Pfeffer, 1992), and so have persisting principals.

Delegating Tasks

Principals told us that the extent to which they shared their responsibilities with others was the best predictor of their ability to run the school effectively over a period of time. This idea is intimately connected to the culture of the school, the principal's assessment of the quality of his or her staff, whether there are additional administrators assigned to the building, their willingness to take on new roles, and their ability to share the burdens of leadership. Even in the face of so many variables, this strategy surfaced as a most reliable one for the principals in our study. If principals were willing to let go, they were usually rewarded with a more involved staff that was also more willing to support the principal's work.

Many principals delegate managerial tasks to eager graduate students or staff members preparing to transition into administrative roles. Principals explained that, although they spent significant time supervising such activities by principal aspirants, it still generally took less of their time than performing the task themselves. Typically, these activities included lunchroom duty, bus and course scheduling, special program organization, data analysis, and textbook ordering. Not only did the interns assist the principals in completing essential managerial tasks, but their presence also promoted professional reflection. As one elementary principal explained: "The intern relationship forces me to slow down and reflect because they ask me questions about why I do what I do and how I decide what I decide."

The irony of using delegation to help manage the balance between instructional leadership and managerial tasks is that even though the principal is desperate to offload activities such as scheduling and budgeting, he or she often winds up sharing pieces of the formal staff evaluation process instead. This is probably true because teachers are usually not equipped or inclined to take on the management side of the principalship, but they do have interest and expertise in instruction. Therefore, many of our principals delegated teacher supervision and evaluation to department chairs, housemasters, teacher leaders, supervisors for pupil personnel services, and assistant principals. This was especially true in larger schools or schools with many new teachers in need of multiple formal observations and write-ups. Although this strategy was extremely useful to principals' budgeting their time, it fell short in facilitating their identities as instructional leaders. Reluctantly, but practically, many principals succumbed.

Emily, an elementary school principal, felt that a shared evaluation model was a worthy trade-off, given all of her responsibilities and the finite number of hours in a day:

> The aides in the school are supervised and evaluated by the special education teachers. I see most of the write-ups, but not necessarily all. Last year I spent entire weekends sitting in front of my computer working on evaluations. My goal this year is to get much better at completing this work during school hours. Delegating some of the responsibility has been very helpful in this regard.

Emily explained that the culture and administrative structure of her school supported the delegation of important work to other staff members, a culture fashioned by the previous principal:

> My predecessor did an excellent job of creating a culture where

it is possible to run a school without a principal. You give
enough respect and responsibility to team leaders, your social
worker, and your administrative assistant. . . . They can reach
you by phone. Some principals feel that they've got to be in on
everything, every meeting . . . that somehow the school would
fall apart without them. These are the folks who burn out.

Emily was not the only principal who felt that a principalship without
significant delegation lacked sustainability. She was also not the only one
who delegated pieces of the evaluation process, even though it was salient
to her professional identity. A successful strategy employed by many
principals was an increased level of participation by teachers in their own
evaluation. As one such principal explained:

I feel like I'm doing all the work, so I've just started asking
teachers to write up some of what they want to work on. This
can work if you eliminate those you may want to terminate.
This way we are working together on improving instruction. I
feel strongly that the teacher should be the change agent, not
the principal.

A different principal said that the balance between being an
instructional leader and having the time for other aspects of her role was
supported in the district by a model that recognizes the distinction between
the needs of the professional-status teachers and the newer staff members.
She suggests that the resulting model provides some relief for the principal
and a more appropriate approach to professional accountability:

The teachers with professional status have a choice to be
evaluated every year or be evaluated every other year. If
they choose every other year, then they have to propose an
alternative project. I do this because, if evaluation is about
professional development, then it makes sense for the best and
most experienced teachers to choose the project themselves. If
the person's performance is "iffy," then I might not give them
the choice even if they have professional status. That's a call I
make as the instructional leader.

In addition to having the best people on board and delegating appropriate
tasks to them, persisting principals also carefully negotiate their schedules
and purposefully structure their time to match their priorities.

Creating the Time for Instructional Leadership by Deliberate Scheduling

In a workday characterized by relentless interruption, a principal who wants to have time for instructional leadership has to create it. Principals from across the country described how they managed their work through the purposeful negotiation of time. For the responding principals, this meant the deliberate allocation of workdays, nights, and weekends to activities as diverse as classroom observations and dinner with professional colleagues.

As days and nights got eaten up with planned meetings and unplanned emergencies, principals realized that instructional leadership activities were too often consigned to nonscheduled time. The design and execution of professional development lacked time slots. Tom, an exasperated middle school principal, gave an example of how the central office not only foists instructional initiatives into his building but also keeps him too busy to provide useful feedback and professional development on the innovation:

> My time is always being invaded, but it's not just my time.
> It's the time you have to actually work with the kids. It's new
> instructional programs that come from the central office. When
> they come in, everyone worries about throwing out the old.
> Block scheduling is a great example. I would like the time
> to work with my teachers and really evaluate whether this
> structure works, but I'm always going to meetings and filling
> out paperwork.

Like Tom, other principals reported spending many hours reacting and precious few reflecting, supervising, and creating. Not surprisingly, principals found that the intentional scheduling of instructional leadership was much more likely to make it happen.

As Lipsky (1981) has described, street-level bureaucrats such as school principals have to find ways to manage huge workloads that reflect their professional priorities. They do so by creating rules about when and where they engage in certain aspects of their work and by maintaining those boundaries without significant regard for the minor catastrophes punctuating the schoolday. This is, of course, easier said than done.

Principals described scheduling activities associated with instructional leadership into the little discretionary time remaining to them after the mandatory building-level and central office obligations. Sometimes it was professional reading relegated to Sunday afternoons, and sometimes it was the scheduling of classroom visitations in datebooks. Other principals made attending grade-level meetings and/or child-study discussions a top priority. Still other principals organized ongoing support groups with like-minded colleagues to share ideas and nurture professional development. Many principals, some literally and some figuratively, are following Lorraine Monroe's (1997) lead of giving themselves time for reflection by entering weekly meetings with fictional people into their datebooks. What was vital to the success of these activities for each of the principals was that the time was sacrosanct.

Creating the Time for Instructional Leadership by Writing Newsletters

Another strategy that principals use to create time for professional reflection and instructional leadership is the writing of weekly newsletters. The principals who equate this activity to instructional leadership compose newsletters with shared characteristics. The pieces are personal, well written, timely, provocative, and focused on teaching and learning, broadly defined. One principal shared a story that he felt illustrated how the newsletter conveys his professional priorities and passions to the school community, thus facilitating his role as instructional leader:

> One of the pieces I wrote that resonated with the community was about an encounter I had with Yo-Yo Ma. You have to understand that Yo-Yo Ma is one of two people in the world who I had a line ready for if I ever got a chance to meet him. I was flying to see my son, and Yo-Yo and his cello were in the seats in front of me. We talked, and at the end of our talk, he told me that being a principal was one of the most important jobs anyone could ever do. He obviously revered teachers and teaching. I wrote about this encounter, my feelings about it, and the reverence with which this most gifted musician held our work and our mission. I got the most fantastic response from parents and teachers. I realized then that I had truly created an audience for my writing. Through the newsletter, I create goodwill and build coalitions for my instructional agenda.

Structured time for the activities of pedagogical leadership was a successful strategy employed by principals for guaranteeing that instruction was not inched out by managerial demands. Principals who knew this and made it happen were far more likely to persist in the role and be satisfied with their work lives. Keeping their eye on instruction enabled principals to recall why they wanted the position in the first place. As was true for Amanda, when principals find ways to keep children, teaching, and learning at the heart of the enterprise, they are able to tip the instruction/management balance in their favor. An elementary principal from the West Coast explained that the "head-teacher role" continues to ground her work and classroom visits continue to provide professional nourishment:

> I have to keep in mind that at the center of it all are the kids. Building a safe and happy place for kids to spend their day and giving them an environment that excites them about learning—that's what I can do here. When I get frustrated, fed up, or off course, I go spend time in a classroom. That is something I would like to do every single day. It just puts it all into perspective and reminds me why I'm here.

Although it is clear that the existing school principalship conspires against an emphasis on pedagogy, the principals in our study were applying several successful strategies to the challenge:

- They hired people who were not necessarily like-minded but who were open-minded and flexible.
- They fostered a school culture that valued shared leadership, group responsibility, and teacher professionalism.
- They prioritized their work and time in order to create opportunities for instructional leadership.

Even when principals successfully employ approaches that afford them time to facilitate improved instructional practice in their schools, they still have to negotiate additional hurdles to their perseverance. One of these challenges is the balance between their personal and professional lives, the focus of Chapter 3.

CHAPTER 3

Negotiating Personal and Professional Balance

Before she came to Massachusetts, Maria Tomas was a school administrator in one of the most challenging districts in Brooklyn, New York. Presently she is a 2nd-year principal in an urban K–8 school in New England. She is married to a lawyer who claims that his working hours are less time consuming than hers. The Tomases have two boys ages 7 and 5. When they first moved from New York, Maria stayed at home with her 2-year-old and new baby.

After remaining at home for several years, she missed her involvement in schools. Finally, she found an administrative position, located a reliable day-care center, and accepted a job offer in a community a great distance from where she lived. Living so far from school proved to be a mistake. In order to pick up the children each day, she needed to leave early. This made her feel guilty and behind in her work, so she sometimes spent weekends at school to compensate. She resented the weekend time spent away from her young sons.

Maria recalled a watershed incident when her son was ill and the day-care teacher phoned to suggest that he be picked up immediately: "I was caught in a snowstorm and it took me 2½ hours to get to him. I was a nervous wreck. When I walked in, the teachers made me feel like I was a terrible mother." That convinced her that if she were to continue working, she needed a job that was closer to home. Her husband was also convinced that, for the sake of achieving a semblance of family life, he needed to make changes at his workplace. He switched departments in his law firm so that he could spend more time at home and less in the office when his son commented one evening, "We don't have a family anymore. Dad also never comes home."

Although not new to the principalship, occupying a new position keeps Maria thinking about work day and night and the increasing demands make her feel that her efforts fall short. There are adult evening programs such as English Language Learning (ELL) and computer classes that use the rooms in the building, sometimes affecting the cleanliness of the school. Lacking more time, Maria finds that she has not made as many contacts with the local community or with nearby university resources as she thinks both desirable and necessary. Unlike her male predecessor, who never left the office, she makes it a point to visit all classrooms: "I don't go the same time every day . . . but I always schedule the visits into my book, varying the roaming time."

Maria has taken direct responsibility for making things happen in her school. If she is pleased, she lets it be known. If she is unhappy, she explains why. She puts everything in writing so that her feelings are clear, and she attributes her bluntness to being a New Yorker. Although when she first arrived, she was persuaded that her assistant principal, a man, got more of a response from custodial staff, she has now found a solution to that problem. The teachers fill out a form listing what needs to be done, and the head custodian responds to the memo. This makes the requests official, and she feels more efficient. In the meantime, Maria is "working to change the sexist culture of the custodial staff [she] inherited." Gender issues at home and in the workplace provided another challenge to Maria's professional vitality and to her personal and professional balance.

OBSTACLES TO LEADERSHIP

Divided Passions

Maria's passion is divided. She knows she is an effective leader. She supports her teachers, includes the families and community in the workings of the school, and still finds time to be a good parent to her own children and, as she said, a "good wife" to her husband. But having to choose between her responsibilities as a principal and as a mother and wife is a tension she constantly faces. When she was at home with her young children, she longed to be back in her professional position. She felt that she was not using her training and expertise as an educational leader to the maximum. Now, finding herself in the principalship, she is aware that she has to make decisions and choices about where her priorities lie. Can she be a good mother and wife as well as a good school leader?

In our interviews with principals and in surveys sent to principals across the country, we found that this tension was part of the life of many of our respondents. Both men and women expressed this. Life circumstances and professional experiences affect the concept of achieving a balance in the principalship. We need to help principals wrestle with this problem. A half-century ago, many cities rarely hired women teachers or principals who were married, thus ostensibly avoiding the dilemma of divided claims on one's time. Clearly that is an even less satisfactory solution today. We need to find ways of building the issue of family balance into the very conception of the principalship in order to generate thinking that would force male and female job-seekers and employers to address it early in one's career, before insuperable problems arise.

Currently, school leadership is an all-encompassing job. Sometimes running a school seems to require the ability to run a small village. Principals are in charge of education, entertainment, infrastructure, legal issues, and after-school activities. Something is bound to go wrong every single day. People who accept jobs like this have to be willing to give something up. The principals in our study indicated that the "something" is frequently part of their personal life. But this can only be a temporary and stopgap measure, which may foster unexpressed resentment and eventually compromise work performance. We asked principals to illustrate how this tension between the professional and the personal looks in their lives and what strategies they use to address the tension between these two passions.

The Impact on Partners and Children

Negotiations Within the Family. In one of our interviews, Brian, a principal in a K–8 school in an urban district, talked about how his wife gave up her position as a music, math, and science teacher in a middle school so that she could stay at home with their three children. She did this in order to make the work easier for Brian. Although she is eager to teach again, she plans to wait until their 4-year-old child, who has some speech problems and follows a special educational plan, is in school all day. Brian acknowledged:

> I couldn't do this job if Carol were not at home. Things that I
> used to do as a teacher with my family, I can't do now. I thought
> I knew what I was getting into, but I couldn't do this job if my
> wife was not at home.

Having his wife give him both physical and emotional support to deal with his work at school as well as personal issues has allowed Brian to do his job with more competence. At this point in the interview, he paused a moment, thought about how hard it was to integrate personal interests with professional life, and said that he ought to bring his wife a bouquet of flowers that evening to thank her for her support. The interview furnished him with an opportunity to reflect on the essential quality that her support provided.

But this is only Brian's point of view. Missing from this conversation is the sacrifice that his wife has had to make in her career. Although that is not part of our concern in this book, we cannot overlook the paradox, illustrated by this case, that one member of this compromise pays a high professional price for relieving pressure on the work life of her spouse.

In another interview, Pam, a principal in a middle school in a suburban community, expressed appreciation for her husband's contribution to their family life:

> My husband was and is extremely supportive of my career as
> an administrator/principal. He took time off to care for the kids

when they got sick, he dropped kids off at school and came
home early so they wouldn't come home to an empty house.

She received the support that she needed, but she indicated how much
she regretted not being available for her children while they were young:
"Kids grow up so fast, and then they go off to college."

These two principals underscored the importance of having someone
in the family providing care for children while they do their job—a strong
indication that it was essential for these principals to have a supportive
"help-mate" who provides assistance in order to do the job well. But it
seems only fair to add that if spouses are willing to adjust their work
schedules to support each other, then job requirements for principals might
be redesigned so that such domestic concessions would be less necessary.
We are losing principals and stressing domestic relationships because we
aren't making these adjustments.

An example is Margery, a former elementary principal, who left
her principal position to become a special education director, a role she
perceived as providing a better balance between being "family friendly"
and being lucrative:

I had a great deal of guilt about returning to work full time after
my first child, but I had little choice. We, as a family, needed the
additional salary to maintain and provide for the necessities
of our lifestyle. I needed a job where I didn't have to work so
many nights.

Margery explained that the additional salary enabled her to send her
son to an independent school that she felt he needed "because of his
shyness. It's taken a long time to find a job that is both professionally
fulfilling and gives me time to be with my family. The special education
director is definitely better than the principalship was." Although she is
licensed to be a principal, Margery has chosen another route to continue
in her profession. She expresses no regret about the change, but one
cannot help feeling that an able leader has been lost from the ranks of
school principals—one more piece of evidence for the crucial need to
rethink the role and the structure of the position that she decided to
resign from.

Margery describes her husband, an administrator in an urban school
system, as simply not able to take responsibility for their children's morning
appointments or emergencies. He is very involved with the pupils in his
school, especially those on the football team whom he describes to her as
having "really tough home lives" and whom he has "adopted," providing
them with additional support. Margery applauds his good works and

dedication but feels the additional family burden on herself and her career at the same time: "Basically," Margery says, "we've come to realize that having children overrules professional promotions because of the time involved for both." Making decisions about handling the tensions between their children's needs and their professional obligations remains a constant focus of negotiation in their family.

How Life at School Enters Life at Home. Some principals, like Brian and Pam, talked about their dependence on spouses, introducing some of the complications that we only hinted at earlier. Margery talked about her husband's reliance on her to pick up more family responsibilities while he was working, even though she was also juggling work pressures. Joe, a middle school principal, talked about how he counted on his wife, who works part time as a psychologist, to assume the necessary family obligations that he is unable to perform. "Am I there, then, for my kids? My wife would say 'no.' We have constant conversations about who is going to take care of the house-related needs. My job simply does not provide the same flexibility as hers." He and his wife have actually entered couples therapy in order to help them sort out the burdens of family and work responsibilities. Although Joe has many stories about his work to tell when he gets home, he is reluctant to talk about them because his wife sees it as yet another intrusion into their privacy. He continues:

> I can't talk about work at home because my wife sees it as an intrusion into our personal life. . . . She resents it in part because she's constantly reminded of my status in the community. On the soccer field, parents talk to her about problems with the school and she instructs them to call me in the office.

His wife claims that as a principal and educator he "always sees issues through a professional lens. My wife feels that because of this I take the side of the teacher when my own son has a school-related issue." This only adds to the pressure of the role. He is constantly put into a position of viewing the education of his own children through the issues he faces in school. Joe observed that his wife sees his using an educational lens as a rejection of his own children.

In addition to the work/personal dilemmas, other demands enter into the conflict. In order to hold her job as a 1st-year principal in a rural community, Joan is required to have a terminal degree. She is presently in a doctoral program at a local university but finds that she is able to work on her dissertation only at night. Joan has twin 3-year-olds and says emphatically, "Family and health issues are number one because if I don't have those, I don't have everything else and my life isn't in place." This requires her to depend on backing from her husband as well as an au pair to help her manage the numerous responsibilities at home and in the workplace.

It was apparent to us that, although male and female principals both indicated a deep concern for their home lives, the women had the major responsibilities for child care, which represented a profound inequity. Whether the principals were men or women, both testified that the women were in charge of providing and/or organizing care for the children. The men assisted, helped, showed appreciation, and gave support, but they did not take the lead. This puts inordinate pressure on female principals, places extra guilt on male principals, and has overall ramifications for the future of the profession and how the principalship is structured. The principalship used to be thought of as a position that a single leader could handle, but based on the stories and reports from the principals whom we interviewed, it looks as if one person for one job may not be sufficient. This is especially true as gender expectations evolve, the role expands, and the lines of authority grow increasingly ambiguous.

How Life at Home Enters Life at School. An elementary principal in the rural Midwest, working with a child whose family was involved with the department of social services (DSS), became very attached to the student and wanted to have her spend Christmas with her and her family rather than be placed in yet another foster home for the holidays. She was ready to provide the student, as well as her own children, with presents for the occasion. Although intent on giving support and affection to the child, she ultimately decided that the best thing to do was to retain her professional position as principal and seek an alternative solution. In an odd inversion, instead of bringing professional concerns home to the family, this principal brought "family" concerns into the school, so that the role of mother momentarily usurped the professional role. All this confirms the difficulty, and often the impossibility, of easily separating the two.

Brian talks to his own children about his school concerns. His son and daughter frequently come to school to visit classes and do special projects with his urban elementary students. These opportunities intersect home life with school life, but they also demonstrate how work responsibilities can impinge on personal ones. Brian told a story about missing a school play that his daughter was in and an award ceremony for his son. He regretted, in retrospect, that he wasn't there to show how proud he was of them.

When asked at the end of the interview if he wanted to add anything, he revealed, "Five years earlier, when I was a classroom teacher, I did not have gray hair." He explained that as a teacher, he was able to designate specific time for his family as well as for his class. As a principal, it was difficult to separate the responsibilities of the two. Ironically, his children were able to find time to visit his school, but he was unable to find time to leave it to attend functions at theirs.

As a matter of fact, home and family frequently enter the school life of the principal. For example, Stan, a very experienced middle school principal in the Northeast, talks about his relationship with his son. He tells how he relies on the advice of teachers in his school to help him manage schoolwork issues at home: "I'm still learning. I learned from teachers how to help my son with chemistry homework."

That realization helped him to discover indirectly that communicating with teachers in his school provided him with resources he needed as a parent. He took that interaction a step further. He reasoned that if he could determine a way to help the families of his students, perhaps he could offer a resource from which he could also benefit. He now runs, with a psychologist, a "fathers' group," which began with five fathers several years ago and now has more than 20 members. This group has continued to meet on a regular basis. Stan believes that every parent is "hungry for honesty and thoughtfulness from the principal about his/her struggles as a parent." The group meetings provide an opportunity to engage in conversations outside the school setting and on a more personal level. But, of course, someone needs to allocate time and schedule opportunities for sharing these important moments. And this makes added demands on already overworked principals.

Allen, a principal in the rural Southeast, told us about issues related to being intimately associated with the community in which he works. An older rule requiring a school leader to live in the same district in which he or she works can hinder as well as facilitate efficiency. Allen maintains, "Sometimes there are pitfalls, but this is the way I do it. My wife claims that our kids could catch negative attention [by living in the community where he worked]." Not being an integral part of the community may provide a distance that helps to balance the personal and professional parts of one's life, but it also separates one from the daily activities of school, introducing a liability that then coexists with an advantage.

When one is unable to separate the professional work from a personal life, the struggle for balance becomes discouraging. A single, female elementary school principal gave this illustration:

> This guy has been trying to ask me out for months and I just
> don't have time. I know he thinks it's personal, but it's not. It's
> the job.

Although she doesn't expressly say so, her pessimism implicitly extends
to her prospects for a social and perhaps even marital future, and this
alone is a serious enough issue to warrant a restructuring of the excessive
time demands of an already taxing position. There are hints here of a built-
in injustice in the system itself.

EFFECTIVE COPING STRATEGIES

Creating Structures

In order to balance the personal and the professional, principals told us
that they must first determine who they are, what they value, and how
their passions could be integrated with their goals. Just as principals
need to dovetail their role as administrator and instructional leader, they
need to decide when to separate and when to integrate their human and
their professional selves. Several principals suggested that scheduling
specific times for the different activities that they must do and establishing
reasonable priorities for what must come first and what can be postponed
help them organize their day.

Some principals managed their lives at work by recording times for
classroom visitations and observations in their appointment book and
holding that time sacrosanct: "Over the course of a week, I get to every
teacher, but I vary the time and day so it doesn't feel as structured as it
really is." A 2nd-year principal explained how she quickly did away with
the open-door policy that she always imagined she would have when
she moved from being a teacher to being a principal: "At first I kept my
book outside of my office and encouraged teachers to sign up to see me
during any available block. My book became completely scheduled. After
that, I set aside specific times during which teachers could come in for
meetings." This is a classic example of how pragmatic discoveries on-site,
as it were, usurped theoretical ideals of how the job ought to be done.
Flexibility in such matters is a crucial feature of responsive and responsible
administrative leadership.

For instance, Ann, a principal in a suburban school, talked about an
assignment in her graduate school class in principal preparation where
she had to read messages sent to her and decide which ones needed to be

addressed first: "I sometimes think about the courses at the university and say what would my professors have done?" This helped her during her first years in the principalship.

In addition to the scheduling of time to accomplish an inordinate number of tasks and address multiple responsibilities, many felt that vacation time provided an important opportunity for regaining a sense of composure and spending time with family. Effective principals find that they are getting better at allocating mental energy for work activities: "All the time that I am here [at school] I think about work. I try not to think about it at home." As we have seen, however, this is not always a matter of choice.

School problems have a tendency to pursue principals beyond their offices and accompany them on the way home. Once they arrive with this extra "baggage," it often proves difficult, if not impossible, to "discard" it. Hence special strategies may have to be developed to escape the unrelenting claims for one's professional attention. One principal and her husband plan trips on weekends because she finds it "a vacation for my head. I tend to come into work on weekends if I'm in town." Ironically, she seems to be saying that one has to create periods of freedom from the work ethic if one is to remain responsible to the claims of one's job.

The Developmental Component of the Principalship

The principal has the obligation of finding the optimal balance among his or her own needs, the needs of individuals in the school, and the needs of the school as a whole. Where a person is in the life cycle and with respect to professional experience play an important part in how work and family will be balanced. Decisions are made based on experience, community relations, and confidence, and this means that new or younger principals might have a lot to learn from their senior colleagues: "It's easier for me to put work first at this time in my life because there aren't any kids or pets at home who need me. When my mother was ill, I did what I had to do at school and then left."

Most of our respondents felt that when there is a crisis at home, that should take precedence and when the crisis is at school, principals are supposed to focus on that first. But a principal's stage in life often dictated his or her response. An East Coast principal explained how she is pulled by competing concerns for her time and emotional energy particular to her stage in life and personal circumstance: "I do my job first; everything else is second. Thank God no one is at home now. My father has Alzheimer's, and it has taken 2 months to get time off to do paperwork to take care of him."

Principal responses were also affected by the length of time they had been in the role and/or in the community. As is true in most work, the longer principals had been in the job, the more efficient they became at getting their work done. They also reported that they felt less scrutinized by the community and better able to enjoy personal time and meet personal obligations. One principal reflected:

> Earlier in my career I took too much work home. It is simply not necessary to do that anymore. Earlier in my career, school always came before home. Now I consider events individually. I've established myself in the community and I have systems in place.

In setting priorities when all issues seem of equal importance, the general consensus was to take care of yourself and your family first. If you do that, you can then take care of everyone else. But as we see from the following remark, such insight can be the result of a slow and painful process of discovery. Bill, with 22 years as a principal and nearing retirement, said:

> I came to realize that the buses rolled before I was born, and they'll roll after I'm gone. I had to realize they were not going to name the school after me, and at the end of the day I had to go home and leave work at work.

Did it require 22 years in the position to realize that? One of the inferences from our research, although we did not ask this specific question, is how many important and useful insights into the role of principal come at the end of a long career, information that could have proved to be of immense value had it been discovered much earlier.

How Coping Strategies Align with Experience

There is an additional developmental component to the principals' responses. As a new principal, you inherit a culture shaped by the former school leader. Your job then is to understand how that came about, gauge its health, and decide how best to shape it through your own prism of awareness. As a beginner in the profession, you might be impulsive, self-protective, conformist, and indeed simply unprepared to face some of the most complicated issues before you. Building trust with the school community becomes the major task for a 1st-year principal. This is especially true for the classroom teacher who has assumed the principalship—moving from teacher to leader. Sharon—first an elementary school teacher, then a curriculum coordinator, then principal of the school—talked about how her predecessor and mentor provided support and assistance when she took the principalship. She said that the former principal "did an excellent job of creating a culture where it was possible to run the school without a principal." She felt that she could follow the model established by prior leadership partly because she had experienced it and partly because of the respect and responsibility that were given to team leaders, social workers, and her administrative assistant in the school.

Conversely, others needed to separate from previous structures and establish their own identity and power to lead. A delicate balance exists between the need to be your own boss and having the confidence to embrace what is best from your predecessor. Unfortunately, insecurity can too easily lead one astray and make depending on previous successful strategies appear to be a sign of weakness.

Certain assumptions lie at the heart of a principal's professional development. A change from teacher to leader, for example, seems significant because it implies that experience and maturity afford principals resources to help restructure schools. But in a discussion of teacher development, Ann Lieberman (1995) complicates this issue: "The two conflicting assumptions about the best way for teachers to learn—either through direct instruction by outsiders or through their own involvement in defining and shaping the problems of practice—stem from deep-rooted philosophical notions about learning, competence, and trust" (p. 592). Like teachers, the new principal is confronted with the challenge of converting this apparent "either–or" choice into a fusion of the best from both options, changing internal and external pressures into sources of inspiration, reservoirs of fresh ideas. It is closely linked to a parallel set of alternatives that need to be reconciled: how to find a way of negotiating expectations of the job with the realities and the culture of the school.

Just as a recent study of surgeons suggested that the success rate of operations was closely related to the experience of the doctors (Mishra, 2003), perhaps the success rate of principals is also related to years of experience. Frequently, however, principals have contracts only for 1 year. And we know that change occurs slowly; perhaps 1 year is not sufficient.

Because the amount of work required in administering a school can be overwhelming, new principals find that they need to listen and learn when they begin in the position. When overwhelmed, principals feel compelled to "micromanage" and to attend everything—after-school activities, school committee meetings, PTO (Parent Teacher Organization) events, community functions, and so forth. One principal tried to justify his need to oversee everything as follows:

> Staff generally don't want a large piece of responsibility for
> running a school—they want validation and respect, they want
> to teach, really. Schools training principals provide a lot of high-
> level theory, but not much nuts and bolts. Being involved in
> community-related activities really helped me understand the
> psychological basis of kids—it helped me develop empathy, a
> crucial quality for a principal to have.

Sharon, entering into a new experience, felt that her prime responsibility was to "get to know the people rather than the job." She discovered that coming into the position with a strong agenda before attaining a full understanding of the culture of the school risked diminishing the effectiveness of any reforms. She wished that when she first entered the position there had been a better structure set up with staff to say, "This is my time, this is your time, let's make this a priority to learn how we can best respect each other's time." It appears that, especially during the early years of a principalship, adjustment to pragmatic realities is as important as dependence on theoretical ideas about sound administrative leadership. Although several of the principals early in their tenure seemed to feel that they needed to be in charge of all situations because that was how strong leaders were supposed to operate, they gradually learned that establishing priorities required them to surrender some of their desire to control. They found that they needed to give themselves permission to take time for personal issues, although this realization came late to some of the school leaders we surveyed:

> Without a firm understanding of myself and my limits, the
> job could easily consume me. I try to keep in mind that,
> although my job is tremendously important, I do not work in
> an emergency ward. Things will get done and solutions will be
> found, but only if all of us go about our business with calmness,
> confidence, and conviction.

Entering her 5th year as a principal, Joan revealed that it took her "4 years of learning [to realize] that it's OK to walk out some days and say I can't deal with that until tomorrow." An understanding husband helps keep her focused as well as balanced. Since he's not in the field of education, he feels comfortable reminding her that there is a life outside the school. Joan acknowledges, "I need to hear that and that's OK." She wishes that there were someone "in upper administration" who was able to communicate that to her. Often, however, such insight can come only from experience rather than from external support.

Setting Priorities

Principals who successfully managed to integrate their personal lives with their professional ones have established strong priorities. One principal said:

> My family is first, no matter what. My husband is the main
> support in my life. I cannot imagine anything, and I include the
> building burning down, that would take precedence over my
> husband and my children. I truly can't.

Since so many principals put their family first, it is a wonder that the commitment and devotion to school is so widespread. Perhaps solving the personal equation actually empowers one to approach the professional task with greater confidence and enthusiasm. In any event, most principals agreed that finding an appropriate structure appeared to help determine the success or failure of effective leadership. If you don't introduce a specific structure into each day, one principal observed, the job can "eat you up alive."

Scheduling one's life and making decisions about how to achieve an appropriate balance is always a challenge, many principals stated. As one principal informed us, "When I work, I work hard. When I play, I play hard. So when I'm in school, I'm there totally." He seems to be able to separate his private life and his professional life and feels that purposeful separation helps balance the two. But Betty, an elementary school principal, plans her life by always being aware of her schedule and thinking ahead:

> I will go to the doctor as soon as something happens at night
> with one of my kids rather than let it go, because I know the
> next day I'm not going to be able to do that. You just think
> you're all set and then something happens and you're not all
> set. That's when alternative plans are essential.

It is clear from the above examples that no template fits all or even most individual conflicts between personal and professional obligations. But it is vital that a keen awareness of potential problems precede a decision to take on the demanding role of school principal. As one principal of a special-needs school told us: "The hours that you work are endless. You don't have much time away from the job." She advises anyone who needs to find ways of "turning off the job" not to make such a commitment. Since she doesn't want to work at home, she sometimes remains at school until 9:00 to get all her work done. Others, however, might find this a totally unsatisfactory strategy.

INTEGRATING PERSONAL PASSIONS INTO PROFESSIONAL LIVES

Both veteran and novice principals told us of their struggles with the middle-management woes documented in the literature: the expectation that they would navigate through huge amounts of work with limited resources, multiple and ambiguous goals, and numerous constituencies (Lipsky, 1981). In order to meet these demands, successful principals fashioned rules that allowed them to address their professional priorities so that their work did not encroach unduly upon their personal lives. For example, they confined working at home to specific hours or days of the week and rarely allowed themselves to deviate from that timetable.

One experienced middle school principal explained how he and his wife "set aside 3 hours every Sunday afternoon for professional reading. We never do this on Friday night or Saturday." For this principal, the separation between work and home needed to be specific and predictable. This provided him with an alternative to busy weekdays with little opportunity for professional development. Others simply held to a more general rule regarding the competing demands of work and home: "When I am at home, I try to focus on home. When I am at work, I focus on work." It may be that the quest for general rules concerning the best way to separate domestic from professional time deflects us from the more productive approach of identifying patterns that work best for particular individuals. But it is difficult to surrender the idea that single solutions exist and to learn to trust the value of private initiatives.

For example, one principal found that walking and reading are essential for her to have a sense of balance. She arrives at school early, parks her car, but does not enter the building immediately. Instead, she takes a short walk to give her time to reflect on the challenges of her upcoming workday. After several weeks, some staff members began to join her and they were able to walk, talk, and discuss problems together. This gave her a way to communicate with her faculty informally and efficiently. It seemed to work well for her and for her staff.

Another principal took a pottery class with her daughter and later related her experiences in that class to teachers from the school. She shared her new skills and her personal story of spending time with her daughter while they were striving to learn something together:

> I'm taking a pottery course right now with my daughter. It's important for me as a person and as a mother. It's also important for my school because I'm modeling. It tells the staff that I will support them in their personal and professional development efforts. It also helps the school to the degree that it helps keep me in balance. (quoted in Boris-Schacter & Merrifield, 2000, p. 93)

Whether one copes primarily through separate or integrated structures, boundaries between the two roles are constantly shifting, fusing, and reforming, and the same may be said of traditional definitions of the role of school principal. According to our data, those most willing to internalize the need for regular redesigning of current concepts of effective school leadership felt the greatest satisfaction with their achievements as administrators.

Unfortunately, however, success at work does not always ensure domestic tranquility. Several principals observed that people at home as well as people at work became irritated when they failed to communicate with each other. We collected considerable data about strained partnerships, couples therapy, divorces, and loneliness. It sounds discouraging to admit that such strains may be an unavoidable consequence of the job in some families. Of course, spousal discontent of this sort is not restricted to the work of school administrators.

A middle school principal in the Midwest, who entered administration as a highly experienced classroom teacher, talks about how he integrates personal interests, including family life, into his professional world. He thinks he has created a replicable model for the school community. "You can encourage staff to bring kids to work—on occasions," he said. "A benefit of having school-age children is that they are part of the community, and you get to be with them in both roles as parent and as a principal."

He is always available for extracurricular activities, so when his daughter, who attended his school, was participating in a track meet, he was there already. He was also one of the few interviewees to stress the importance of keeping in good physical shape: "For a while I used yoga to learn how to be a school principal." But in spite of these strategies, he confessed that he was constantly preoccupied with school: "I can be with my family, and not really there. I have had to learn how to disconnect in my head." To accomplish this, he has trained his administrative team to do some of the job without him.

It is easier for this to happen in secondary schools, since few elementary schools have the resources to support such administrative teams. In addition, the principal we are discussing has held his job for many years. This has allowed a bond of trust to grow between him and his staff: The staff can take initiatives without constantly seeking approval from the principal, and the principal knows that he has reliable co-workers who do not require constant supervision.

A NEW MENTORSHIP FOR ALL PRINCIPALS

A question asked by many when taking on the duties of principal is: "How I can do what I feel is essential to my mission as an educational leader without compromising my family responsibilities?" Our study respondents indicated that a period of transition between the classroom and the principalship could provide support as they are learning the job. The feeling is that an internship is valuable but does not provide enough experience. During the internship, responsibilities of school leadership still lie with the principal, and there is always assistance during the transition period. Perhaps what we need is an "advanced internship" where the new principal is mentored by an experienced current principal or by a retiree. Instead of having this mentorship focused on the traditional fare of record-keeping, test-score analysis, and coping with difficult parents, it should be focused on the creation of a healthy life balance that leads to sustainability.

Since principals need to effectively support teachers with their professional growth, deal with parental desires and issues, respond to the superintendent and the school committee, and still champion the students' learning and care, they require the same reinforcement that they give to others. Therefore, in addition to supportive internships for new principals, we should also consider ways to encourage those who remain in the position for longer periods. One of the hardest things about being a principal is realizing the difference between your own perceptions of what the job is about and the expectations of your staff and community.

GENDER MATTERS

Gender and level of experience frequently make a difference in the reception of a new principal. One woman principal said that her actions and choices differed from those expected in the prevailing school culture. She struggled to be effective in both traditional ways and ways that seemed true to herself: "I came here because I wanted to provide instructional leadership—I'm good at it, and that was my mandate from the superintendent. But the staff was looking for someone who'd provide them with more care and support—maybe because I'm a woman." When her style of leadership proved different from that of her predecessor, who was a comrade to all, she was criticized for not tending to the emotional needs of her staff. Pam, an elementary principal, says:

> I like the fact that my job lets me deal with all the members
> of a community—parents, kids, teachers. I can see my efforts
> more directly here. Change is not only possible; I can see it
> happening. That's the positive side of this job.

Another principal, when asked about integrating personal and professional life, said, "I think that you have to be able to dovetail who you are into— and what you value into—what you stand for as an administrator." She uses to her advantage the fact that she is not only a principal but also a mother of three children. She will say to a parent, "I know that I am not going to put your child in a position that is an unhappy position or that I might regret or that you might regret." She and others find that the principal needs to create the climate of the school. By sharing the personal as well as the professional, a principal helps define a culture that values that integration.

The analysis of our data indicates that there are gender differences in two respects: There are fewer women principals with children living at home, and women principals have less experience in the role than the men in the sample. We concluded that the women, unlike the men, wait to enter demanding administrative jobs until their children are older and they have more teaching experience. It is clear from our data, as is generally true in society, that women still bear the brunt of child-care responsibilities and tend to feel that they must have more experience before moving into administrative roles. This has a major impact on whether and when women enter the principalship and how they perform their tasks and cope with stress while in the role.

SHARING INFORMATION THAT PERSONALIZES RELATIONSHIPS AND BUILDS CAPITAL

Several principals use newsletters and e-mails to talk to their constituency and provide them with information about themselves. The newsletters frequently tell stories of personal feelings as well as giving school information. A high school principal tells his staff and community about a family skating trip. He then continues to remind the staff about the faculty variety show. By providing personal information to the school community, he touches on his human qualities, attempting to bridge the gap between the personal and professional. Another principal reveals feelings of exhaustion to newsletter readers. Undoubtedly, some principals would find this risky, fearing that the teachers and parents would think he was a complainer. Obviously, this principal feels that he has earned the right to share these thoughts:

> From my very small vantage point, as I approach my personal
> landmark of being a half-century old, I am left with few
> sweeping insights. The routines and maintenance requirement
> of daily life leave my sagging body drained and my mind stuck
> with the mundane problem of selecting what I am willing to
> forgo on my ever-lengthening "must do today" list.

A different middle school principal describes how he uses the newsletter he writes to lighten the emotional burden associated with the work:

> The hardest part for me is that at some level, you're responsible
> for everything that goes on here. Every day some kids go
> home unhappy. I don't know how to get rid of this piece. The
> newsletter has been a way for me to combine my personal
> stance and apply it to my life as a principal, because the column
> I write is more personal than professional.

SEEING BALANCE IN PERSPECTIVE

Maria, as well as the other principals we interviewed, searched for ways of maintaining a life while performing their professional responsibilities. Granted, some days one commitment superseded the other, but the principals developed strategies that established a manageable balance between the two. Of course, "manageable balance" has no absolute meaning and, in fact, may imply a different lifestyle and work style for each individual describing it. Some simply accepted that, for a large part of their career, school demands would occupy a major portion of their lives. Others scheduled regular family time and refused to allow school problems to usurp it. Some lapsed into work rhythms that found school challenges more satisfying than domestic ones. Others found in their spouses and children or any other domestic arrangement a fulfillment that was not equaled on the job, however gratifying it seemed. Of course, as we all know, such tensions are not restricted to the field of education. The first step in clarifying such dilemmas is to be aware of them. This means that recognizing the need is more important than how that need is articulated. Indeed, in our interviews and surveys, we discovered that the most energetic principals were those constantly conscious of their problems and able and willing to express and discuss them.

CHAPTER 4

Negotiating Community Expectations and Personal Definitions of Effective Leadership

Linda Josephs began her professional career as a classroom teacher in a large urban school system in the Northeast. Her ability to reach her students effectively as well as work collaboratively with her colleagues was soon apparent. It wasn't long before she assumed a leadership role mentoring new teachers and starting a program for gifted children in her school. The program for gifted children proved to be a prototype for other schools in the city. Children whose potential had previously been neglected were provided curricula and activities that motivated them to achieve higher levels.

Partially based on her gifted program initiative, the school system recognized Linda's leadership potential and soon she found herself in the central office as curriculum coordinator. When the need arose for a principal in one of the schools, she proved to be the best candidate. Years in the school system and the respect of colleagues and the superintendent provided her with the support she needed to create new programs, select innovative curricula, and hire appropriate staff. It was a time when school-based management was widespread. But as the years passed, the political situation changed and so did pressures on the principal.

After 10 years of success, Linda felt the need for new challenges, and when she was offered the principalship in an elite suburban school nearer to her home, she accepted the position. However, even though proximity to her home and family remained a benefit, the bureaucratic interventions she had hoped to escape in the urban setting were still evident. The state adopted new curriculum frameworks and new standards for student achievement that increased pressures on classroom teachers as well as on the principal. She and her teachers felt obliged to alter the present school curricula to follow statewide frameworks so that students could succeed in the mandated tests.

Many parents were confused and alarmed about the assessment changes. Much of Linda's professional time was diverted from classroom visits and teacher support in order to appease these community concerns. During her principalship in the urban school, Linda had been free to provide support for both staff and students. She had had some central office mandates, but for the most part she was allowed to run her school independent of influences from various constituencies. The principalship, like teaching, is a service occupation. Built into the position is the idea of contributing to the lives of others and improving the educational environment for all involved, but at the suburban school Linda felt pulled in too many different directions.

She felt the additional pressure of parental demands, which had been less apparent in her previous appointment in the urban school. Since elementary principals are so closely associated with all areas of school operation, Linda felt that her responsibilities are visible, comprehensive, and demanding. Trends toward higher standards as measured by test scores and decentralization of decision making for schools, combined with the move toward school-based management, placed even greater pressure on her. Suggestions by educational researchers encouraging greater involvement of parents, the business community, and teacher empowerment forced Linda to give parents more responsibility and a greater voice in school decisions. The sorts of school decisions that Linda had made earlier, which had been respected and endorsed by the community, were now being questioned. She felt her authority eroding. Linda explained that her early retirement was precipitated by intervention from outside groups into the everyday functioning of the principalship. The loss of autonomy and community respect did not seem worth the hard work and increasing pressure.

DEFINING THE COMMUNITY

In determining the effect that the community has on schools, we asked principals how they define and respond to community concerns. The principals told us that their clearest path to success was the articulation of the mission to those with an interest in the schools. They described the community as including parents and guardians, teacher unions, and school committees and state organizations.

OBSTACLES TO LEADERSHIP

Pressure from Parents, Unions, and Central Office

In previous chapters we talked about decisions that principals make between work and family priorities. These tensions continue to be present, but today's principal must face the additional problem of balancing school needs with community demands. There may have been a time when docile parents accepted the priorities principals established for their pupils and trusted them to carry them out fairly and effectively, but this is no longer the case. Parents may once have attended PTO (Parent Teacher Organization) meetings to listen; today they come to speak. Many principals, who once presided, now attend these meetings with "pad in hand." Perhaps we exaggerate, but we do so to make a point. The voice of the community is awake in the educational landscape and it deserves to be heard, but principals aren't always prepared for the public's participation.

Linda's unease was not unique among our respondents. An elementary school principal explained:

> A concern I have is the parent community. We have an active
> parent group, which I welcome, but they expect a lot. I have ideas
> about how we meet standards and sometimes the parents have
> different ideas. They are more focused on enrichment. It is hard
> to meet their expectations when my priorities may be different.

The parents in her community wanted the school curriculum to focus more on enrichment than the principal deemed appropriate. The principal needed to make certain that the students in her school successfully met the measurable goals for improvement based on standardized tests. As is now true for most principals, the question facing her is how to meet the state mandates and still encourage teachers to provide an interesting and challenging curriculum for all students. This requires the principal to be an instructional leader who works with teachers to ensure that the curriculum contains motivating activities and provides support for student success in the state tests. It is a full-time job.

Many principals stated that much of their job required them to do other work, so that there was not enough time left to give the support and motivation for helping teachers fulfill their instructional obligations. Linda describes the impact of the union as an additional complicating factor that sometimes interferes with her addressing parental concerns regarding academic goals: "One of the things I didn't like [in the urban school] was the force of the union and the sense of clockwatching." Although we expected other references to unions when we asked about community influences on the principal, Linda's comment was the only one we received. She felt that union regulations restricted her teachers from performing some of their daily responsibilities.

Linda felt that she was able to help her students and teachers realize their potentials early in her career. She led her schools by responding primarily to the students' interests and abilities. However, seemingly endless directives, dispatches, and competing initiatives distracted her and other principals from this essential task. When the pressure comes

from outside the classroom—from parents, unions, and central office—
authority no longer lies solely with the principal.

Frequently, administrative support for issues that confront the
principal in her own school diminishes while responsibilities for dealing
with community issues increase. Michael, a high school principal from
the East Coast, described how the endless and competing directives are
experienced: "It's hard to stay focused on why I got into this crazy business
in the first place. You're being pulled in so many different directions that
you have to remind yourself why you're here."

When Stakeholders Have Different Goals

As the teacher becomes more and more accountable for student
performance, pressure is placed squarely on the principal to encourage
the teachers to urge their students to perform well on tests. Such higher
accountability may, on balance, be an advance for public education, but
the principal is caught in the classic middle-management bind of having
responsibility without commensurate authority. When schools consider
successful performance in exams as the essential ingredient for the
effectiveness of programs, many innovative curricula are sidelined and
classroom time is filled with test preparation. Alan, a veteran elementary
principal, described it this way:

> It's difficult keeping abreast of the current "trends" in our
> trendy profession in which the pendulum swings so vastly.
> Also, balancing personal and professional obligations and the
> time in which to do both. Perhaps my most major challenge is
> facing the fact that there will always be loose ends, always be
> more work than can be done, realizing that I cannot reach every
> child, accepting the things I cannot change, and dealing with
> unprofessionalism from professionals.

The pendulum has swung once more in response to the federal
No Child Left Behind legislation. Community and school expectations
have moved closer to the federal mandates, which have narrowly
defined competence as successful test scores. As David Driscoll (2004),
Massachusetts Commissioner of Education, has written, "When someone
begins a diet but doesn't give up chocolate and fried foods, he can't blame
the mirror when he keeps gaining weight. The mirror—like testing—only
reflects the whole, true picture" (p. 43). Educators rightfully argue that the
test is not necessarily the whole, true picture. The high-stakes nature of
testing is often inappropriate because too many variables affect student

test performance. Among these variables is the fact that school districts have inequitable resources, putting some students at a disadvantage.

With community involvement reflecting the strong concerns of so many constituencies regarding test scores, the resulting demands play a role in changing the responsibilities of principals to keep the community informed. Schools fare better when the community is actively aware of what is happening in the school. Schools should satisfy a community's reasonable expectation that they provide meaningful information on how they are performing and that they act responsibly and in the students' best interest.

When parents' desires clash with teachers' desires, or when one teacher's conviction runs counter to that of another teacher or of the principal, tensions ending in competition and territorialism become evident. On the other hand, schools can thrive when they reflect on and honor these differences. Often in such schools, tensions can become sources of creation. Meeting all these challenges requires the principal to have strategies that incorporate the ones that will benefit the school while setting aside some of the others. Competent principals know this and are trained to operate collaboratively. One experienced principal, Grace, described ways in which she meets the challenge:

> I have had to learn to work with and through disturbances, distractions, and interruptions; that my professional life should be lonely; understand that when I speak, people listen; to make sure I know what I'm talking about; and *not* to think out loud. I have had to learn to listen more effectively. I have also learned that patience is certainly a virtue and one that needs practicing much more often. I've had to adopt the strategy of delegating and have had to hone the related skills that go with that strategy. I've learned the strategy of consensus and [am] opposed to unanimous votes. I've learned that I need to be a role model and do as much as I can do while expecting as much as I expect.

Challenges to Collaboration

The ability to work in a group and elicit contributions from and offer support to each member creates a positive environment for everyone. Many women in leadership roles have adapted to a life deeply rooted in the collaborative world, and this helps them to adjust from classroom teaching to leadership in education. Principals in our study agree that their role requires a collaborative spirit. In addition to becoming advocates of their own ideas, they feel that they must listen and respond to the community around them. One female principal in our study observed:

> I think my authority comes primarily from four different places.
> I think probably the strongest amount of authority comes
> from relationships. The building of relationships and all of the
> skills that are required to do that. Paying attention to people,
> listening to people, observing classrooms, giving suggestions,
> relationships. The stronger my relationships are with teachers
> and parents, the more influence I have.

Of course, when schools are not providing adequate leadership and students are not achieving, other measures must be taken. A recent report describes how a group of parents in a community with low-performing schools banded together in order to instigate improvement in one of the schools. They were able to change the leadership and dismiss several teachers who were ineffective. Although they say that the school is still housed in a decrepit building with missing books and outdated equipment, they sense that they have initiated the change they feel is needed for their children to improve and prepare for the future. Without the input of these parents, the status quo within the school would have remained. This kind of community pressure helps leadership to provide for improvement. The principals in our study indicated that they depended on cooperation with parents and community members in order to make their schools run more efficiently and effectively. Sharon, an elementary principal, concluded:

> I like the fact that my job lets me deal with all the members
> of a community—parents, kids, teachers. I can see my efforts
> more directly here. Change is not only possible; I can see it
> happening. That's the positive side of this job.

When disagreements arise, principals are forced to add to their multiple responsibilities the role of negotiator. This is the most difficult task of all, since courses on how to negotiate with dissident community members are rarely included in the training of school administrators. As in other professions, educators need to expand their vision of requirements for preparing future leaders in the field. In spite of the absence of such preparation, and very much to their credit, the most successful principals in our study have been able on their own to devise strategies for turning disagreements with the surrounding community into reasonable and enlightened policy.

Cultural Dissonance: Race and Gender

In one case Audrey, a Black principal who came to a predominately White suburban school system after many successful years administering in an urban school with mostly Black students, talked about how difficult it was to reach the families in the new community. She said that when she began, the White community was suspicious of her and "scrutinized [her] every move." They had assumptions about how she would behave, what she would know, what she would emphasize, and how intellectually capable she was.

Since she had been an urban principal prior to coming to this school, the new community was concerned that she would have difficulty providing the leadership required in the suburbs. While teaching and during her first principal position, Audrey and a group of women educators met once a month in someone's kitchen to discuss pedagogical issues and do administrative housekeeping. Although the meetings lasted only a year, they provided much support. She explained that although race exacerbated the community's lack of confidence in her, it was her gender that challenged her confidence in herself. Some of her concerns are reflected in this statement:

> I'll bet that you hear this from most women. We're afraid
> people will find out about us. We're making decisions about
> lives—about retention. Who died and made me expert? We're
> determining programs—even placement is scary. Sometimes
> we determine whether a kid will live with his parents, whether
> parents will get money for programs. I think men are more
> confident. [Women are] raised to second-guess [them]selves. We
> make decisions based upon our intelligence and think that it's
> based upon our emotions. Women are just less secure and more
> concerned with how everybody else feels.

One of the toughest hurdles that principals have to face is the ingrained prejudices about leadership that preoccupy members of the community before the arrival of a new administrator. A dual problem ensues: A new principal must reeducate the community about the flexibility of his or her ideas and educational qualifications even as a community tries to "educate" the principal about its fixed expectations. This becomes even more complex when a Black principal comes into a White school and vice-versa.

People of color and women—who are still seen as atypical in the principal's role—are frequently viewed with a more critical eye by their constituency. Whether anticipated or not, this can become one more unwelcome obstacle in the path of an eager and well-trained administrator whose only interest is in doing his or her job well.

Women who enter the principalship after teaching many years face other issues. Sometimes—and this is not always apparent to the outside community—the image of the last principal haunts the current leader. Long-standing, male-dominated leadership can give special meaning and security to teachers and to the community. Some of the women principals we interviewed complained about the difficulties of entering the role when the present culture of the school was infused with prior cultures. One principal said: "The previous principal took care of all the teachers and he bellowed in the office. Teachers and parents don't come to me. They were accustomed to his style and his just making things happen."

Another female principal described her role as "a philosophical queen, a benevolent dictator, and a good parent all at the same time." It is clear from these brief observations how much of the principal's task must be learned on the job rather than before assuming it. Both parents and new principals must be ready to abandon some of their prior fixed notions about how to run a school and who is best qualified to run it. They must also be willing to accept a pragmatic challenge that demands an almost daily role redesign and cultural accommodation.

State and Federal Mandates

A major area of pressure from the community on schools comes from federal and state mandates affecting classroom instruction and curriculum. "As the field of special education becomes more complicated and more litigious, principals are under increasing pressure to know the laws relating to special education and to know how to implement them at the school level" (Davidson & Gooden, 2001, p. 42). Increasing numbers of students have been identified as having special education needs, and teachers require more support to provide for them. More than any other area in public schools, special education is entangled with and affected by a variety of complex issues. The rigorous demands for compliance with the Individuals with Disabilities Educational Act (IDEA) have placed heavy administrative burdens on building-level administrators, including such tasks as excessive documentation and record-keeping. State and local school districts are responsible and held accountable for providing supervision, management, and administration of special education services. One experienced principal found that so much of his time was spent learning and applying the legal implications of the district's mandates, writing reports, and scheduling appropriate services that this work took precedence over other tasks. He shared his feeling with us:

> A big part of this job is now about special education. I spend a huge amount of my time in team meetings, CORES [special education evaluation meetings], working with service providers, etc. So a grounding in special education law and knowing your district's SPED system is crucial. If I had to pick one thing to change, it would be to have an associate principal in charge of SPED in each building. It's a huge drain for the principal.

The level of knowledge of special education law could ultimately affect the type of leadership a principal demonstrates in the management of educational programs and services for students with disabilities. If the knowledge of special education law is minimal, it could have a rippling effect on all parties involved. Without the knowledge and understanding of special education law, managing the program could become frustrating and burdensome for the administrator. Special education law is one example of a federal mandate to which the principal and schools need to respond. Furthermore, since special education law changes so frequently, school systems must recognize the need to provide ongoing staff development in this area.

The No Child Left Behind Act is another mandate requiring special attention. Everyone takes notice (including realtors) when local newspapers list the schools that did not pass the federal requirement for improvement. This puts the schools and the principal on a federal "watch" list. The principal is now accountable to constituencies in addition to students, teachers, parents, central administration, and policymakers. Given that accountability, the job has become almost too much for one person. Powerful and relevant education for all students is something that everyone wants. How we acquire the means for achieving that is what frequently divides the public and subsequently becomes counterproductive. This introduces another opportunity to connect the schools to the community and the community to the schools. Parents have a right to be heard. If there are low expectations on the part of teachers, principals need to be aware of it. Principals in our study acknowledged an unavoidable need to address this issue with teachers, students, and parents. As with special education laws, an in-depth understanding of the results of testing children is essential for the principal in order to help teachers plan an appropriate curriculum that meets the aims of No Child Left Behind without ignoring other desirable educational goals.

The Pressures of Testing

Testing students has become an integral part of the work of schools. Although the kind of assessment we do reflects what we value, everyone involved in the process doesn't necessarily share the same values. Most principals agreed that a desirable curriculum would balance knowledge, skills, creativity, and civic activity. Testing only for knowledge is limiting. But as one educator warns, "It is naïve to believe that high-stakes tests are going away. Therefore, it is the role of professional educators to fashion a school environment that works within a political reality that defines teacher accountability as a single test score" (Boris-Schacter, 2001, p. 47). Since at present this "political reality" cannot be ignored, the assiduous principal will have to learn to accept it and resist it at the same time. The problem extends to the fundamental question of grading. In his weekly newsletter to faculty, parents, and the community, one high school principal writes:

> Often, we get a perspective for students' overall performance based upon the grades we issue as teachers, but this view is not necessarily the one shared by your colleagues or your students. By next week I should have an opportunity to receive schoolwide reports for the percentage of different letter grades issued as a school, and then the percentage of letter grades issued by individual departments. Department heads will be issued reports detailing the percentage of different letter grades issued by individual teachers. A periodic review of our grading practices is important so that we have similar standards and expectations in similar courses. I encourage you to engage in this conversation and practice with your colleagues in the days ahead.

This high school principal uses the newsletter to provide guidance to teachers and to speak to the community in general. In it he is encouraging his faculty to collaborate with colleagues and to articulate similar standards and expectations in their various courses. He is initiating a dialogue with parents and teachers about how assessment will help them understand the progress of students.

Community Expectations in Addition to Those of the Bureaucracy

The public frets about whether our children today are becoming good people. When there is delinquency and disrespect on the part of youth, the public holds schools largely responsible for remedying these troubles.

Educators influence students' moral development but not solely by being good role models. They need to learn from their own limitations and continually develop their capacity to see the perspective of every child in the class. But embracing diversity, whether the subject is conduct or learning, can be discouraging to a teacher who measures success by consensus rather than diversity. All this means is that principals need to view their leadership role from multiple perspectives. Teachers who think that they can no longer make a difference in students' lives become disillusioned and feel that their role as agents of change is diminished. That is when principals need to provide support to help teachers master their ability to work through discouraging moments, create opportunities for them to use their talents, and have a greater impact on students' lives.

But even this is easier said than done. When a school leader becomes disillusioned, the entire school suffers. In a *New York Times* article, Sara Rimer (2002) described one principal who said she had been exhausted, frustrated, and finally defeated by the state system's bureaucracy, which left her without enough teachers and with entrenched union rules that kept her from meeting with her teachers. Her focus was to change aspects of the school, but that was not foremost in the minds of the teachers and parents. Such a disconnect between a school leader and her staff inhibits collaboration and limits progress.

EFFECTIVE COPING STRATEGIES

Looking for Balance

As the principals in our study took on additional tasks, they needed to delegate some of their responsibilities to others. Determining which tasks are essential and must be addressed immediately, which can be postponed, and which can be delegated to others takes much experience and thought. One principal said:

> How do we get a better balance? I don't know if that can
> happen because the expectations of the community won't
> change. How do we change their thinking? It takes time,
> patience, and planning. Everyone always demands to see the
> principal, even when we know it isn't necessary. We need to
> change the culture that depends so much on one person.

Time, patience, and planning! That is what most principals are concerned about when administrative details interfere with the work that needs to be done to provide services to both staff and students. Persistent principals kept up with the reports about schools and schooling that appear in the local media. This provided them with up-to-date information about what emphasis on education is influencing parents and other community members. Just as principals need to be informed about what the community is feeling, they also need to communicate their ideals and goals to the families and communities. It is precisely this give-and-take that moves a school's educational agenda forward.

Forming Coalitions

Many of the principals we interviewed and surveyed used bulletins sent home to families to explain to the community their programs inside the school. They hoped that this information would help change the perception of academic procedures and what the priorities were for the faculty. One principal wrote in a newsletter to parents:

> One of my concerns about the recent changes in the state curriculum frameworks and the ever-changing [state tests] is that they represent a backing away from teaching for understanding to a more simplistic teaching of "basics." It mirrors the periodic rhetoric that states that the problem of our schools is that we don't teach phonics. Basic skills—which obviously include phonics—are vitally important to learning. However, learning that starts and stops with basic skills and doesn't move to comprehension and to problem solving leaves middle school students with no skills at all.

This principal highlights one of the major controversies in schools today. Newsletters such as the one above not only give information about programs and events in the school but also clarify the thinking that frames the school's goals in an effort to bring the population outside closer to an insider's understanding of the principal's philosophy. This communication is essential. The newsletter is a vehicle for communication, but it also shapes the community's expectations of the principal, builds capital for future disagreements, and facilitates the idea that everyone is in this together. As principals spend more and more time responding to community demands and suggestions, their work has expanded from the more limited view of the parameters of the job that they envisioned when entering the profession.

When an adversarial climate among teachers, students, and parents persists in schools, principals are prevented from achieving desired goals. Conflict among all the constituents only leads to diminished education for the students. How a principal responds to this situation and negotiates solutions will almost certainly affect—and should aim to improve—the school environment. The leader who uses a direct approach and enlists the support of all groups can create positive solutions. To move from individual to collective decision making, a principal needs to engage in collegial conversations about the school, its purpose, its beliefs, and its problems. Often these analytical (and difficult) conversations are the only means to decide whether a habitual practice is the best way to achieve the shared vision of the school. One principal explained her ideas:

> I believe that what I would have wanted to do is start off getting to know the people rather than the job, which I don't know if that's even humanly possible. But I say that because it would have saved me probably 4 years of learning. One of the hardest things about your first principal job is realizing the difference between your expectations and ideas of what the job is about, and the expectations of your staff and community.

Principals insisted on the importance of continuing to maintain open communication in order to provide better services and support for the students. Parents sometimes claim that schools undermine their authority. Perhaps they do, because education is meant both to implement old skills and open the mind to new ideas. While some parents feel that schools are sabotaging their family values, others are delighted that schools are reinforcing them. Another principal observed the centrality of political savvy to successful leadership:

> I've been prepared by my prior positions that allowed me to think about the importance of engagement with faculty and parents. I learned how to respect teachers, and that supports learning. Living in this school system for 20 years, I could get it to work for me politically. You [as principal] have to see the political picture.

Does this mean that principals need to be politicians, too? There is no agreement on this issue, but it would be a mistake to underestimate the power of diplomacy as a tool of persuasion in negotiating policy with various constituencies involved in the educational process. Failure to exercise diplomacy can so alienate some groups from each other that reaching consensus becomes an unachievable goal.

A classroom teacher may respond to community demands differently from the principal. Teachers talk to parents and try to adapt curriculum and experiences to meet the needs of individual children. The principal, however, must engage every component of the organization to focus on objectives that support the whole school as well as the child. He or she must examine how these goals are met for everyone in the school—students, teachers, bus drivers, curriculum designers, administrative assistants, special education directors, and food service workers.

Although this is not an easy task, it is a necessary one. Principals need to hear from the community and react intelligently to their concerns. Just as the philosophy of those who believe that schools should be run by strong principals is based on the belief that teachers left unsupervised will do as little work as possible, if the same attitude were embraced by principals in regard to members of the community, little would get accomplished. The culture of the school is largely determined by how the principal responds to the community's issues. The principal who is able to respond effectively can shape new cultures, and that can result in cooperation by community members. Good principals have been able to convince resistant members of the community and move members away from a narrowly defined conception of school success such as test scores.

The principal as cultural authority—which years ago meant a White man with graying hair in a suit, usually sitting in an office behind a desk— is no longer the image one sees in schools. He used to be considered the patriarch who controlled the students, observed the teachers, and met with the parents. He was perceived chiefly as a symbolic leader (Deal & Peterson, 1999). Unfortunately, this attitude is not completely extinct. Frequently, principals condemned what they saw as persistent but antiquated community expectations that they devote inordinate amounts of time to being at the school and at school-related activities. One principal commented on her community's expectation of constant availability and access:

> I feel pessimistic about the community changing its expecta-
> tions of the principal. I think if any change were to come
> about, it will take time and planning. Everyone who calls the
> school wants to talk directly to the principal, even when they
> don't need to.

It is clear that in order to keep excellent people in leadership roles, we need to rethink what we require of the principal. Whether we like it or not, in the current milieu of expectations, reeducating one's constituencies has been added to the main task of principals—educating one's students.

Keeping Students at the Heart of the Enterprise

Of particular importance is one bit of evidence that emerged from our interviews and surveys about a question we never asked. Regardless of the preponderance of complaints regarding how hard the job was, principals never complained about the students in their schools. They emphasized providing for the success of all students— success not only in test scores but also in creativity, reasoning, and powerful, relevant education. They felt that they could achieve that when they were not inundated with massive regulations coming from community mandates. It is the students that motivate outstanding principals. As one described his feelings:

> Another way to understand what makes the job "doable" is to understand the personal joy of being a principal. It comes mostly from the kids, watching them grow and succeed, but it also comes from seeing the staff interact with each other and with the kids. When I'm in my building, in classrooms, waiting for the buses, or at activities, seeing the kids is what fills me up and makes the work not a burden but a joy.

Linda Josephs found that too many administrative details prevented her from doing the job the way she had hoped she could. Like Amanda, she was convinced that mandates from state departments of education and the federal government requiring frequent testing of children and writing reports to political constituencies forced her to spend too much time and energy away from her role as instructional leader. Linda's decision to retire early was an indication of how she was finally defeated by the state system's bureaucracy.

Other principals manage to stay. If the tension is between instructional leadership and community demands, how do principals successfully negotiate that tension? If educators move into the principalship in order to fulfill the role of instructional leader, then how do they organize the overwhelming time demand of activities such as meeting with and responding to parents, the community as a whole, the state and federal mandates? As was true for each of the tensions the principals faced, we found that many of the principals we interviewed and surveyed were able to cope through negotiation. In dealing with community issues, principals were able to remain effective when

- They successfully negotiated with the central office personnel to participate in hiring building-level staff.
- They successfully negotiated the delegation of tasks to others.

- They successfully negotiated their schedules so that there was specific time for personal activities.
- They used frequent communication to the families and the community to provide information about the school and to shape the community's expectations of the work of the schools.

Hiring the Right People and Delegating Tasks

The best teachers have the best leaders. Those principals who had more autonomy to hire quality personnel gave more autonomy to their teachers. Having competent staff to support the students, principals were able to provide more flexibility to teachers to help students achieve on tests and in many other areas. They found that the best way to help students do well in school was through complex educational experiences rather than test preparation. With autonomy around staffing, creativity, and budget decisions, successful principals were able to provide support for bringing out the best in their teachers. Many factors help to shape a successful school, but without a creative principal, it can't be done.

In addition to hiring appropriate teachers and staff members, principals described creating a different culture in the schools. They sharpened their communication and observational skills and used them to inspire some teachers to find more effective ways of reaching their students. They emphasized advancing teachers because of perceived potential rather than only because of past achievement, and they trusted them to provide teacher leadership.

Since the knowledge base was developing so quickly, one principal could not possibly be an expert on everything. Instead of being discouraged by this fact, successful principals were able to delegate some responsibilities to others in the school without feeling that their authority was being compromised. They were able to expand their influence and power by surrendering some to others. These principals provided shared decision making and shared leadership. By doing so, they not only lightened their workload but also improved the academic experience of students and the professional development of teachers.

Making Time for Personal Nurturance

In spite of the huge demands on principals, our interviewees spoke repeatedly about connections between their work and their personal interests and lives. An elementary school principal told stories about his frequent trips to antique shops to find old books. These books are on display on a bookshelf in his office, and he reviews them occasionally to reflect on how schools were run "in the olden days." It puts things in perspective for him. Another principal said, "I need to read and I need to have love in my life. I think it's healthy to have something else going on." Another talked about skiing every weekend. She said, "It is a vacation for my head."

On the question of integrating personal and professional lives, several principals described how spirituality entered into their work. One principal said: "I know I have a value system that has been instilled in me and I carry it with me. I have a religious background, and my religion means a lot to me, and I think that helps me in many situations." Another said: "In a few weeks I will be an ordained deacon. It fills me up in a different way. It makes it easier for me to come back to work on Monday morning."

But not everyone spoke about spirituality as connected to religion. Some spoke about it as a step toward understanding and fulfilling themselves, but not necessarily by themselves. The principal previously mentioned, who together with her daughter explored a new experience, later was committed to sharing her learning with others. The experience was important for her as a person and as a mother, but it was also a way of modeling relationships to members in her school. She first internalized her insight, then found a way of expressing it to others: "Pottery reminds me of the power of the aesthetic and the kinesthetic, and it is an activity that one does in silence. I am professionally developing my ability to be silent."

Some of the readings that another principal told us about fostered a spiritual side of her life. She said, "What has really helped me think about using my time is having read *Leading with Soul* by Lee Bolman and Terrence Deal. The book reminded me to nurture the spiritual side and keep what is important at the core." These principals allotted time for themselves and found that it was easier to return to their professional worlds having had the "spiritual respite." The break from the rigors of leadership had provided them with renewed energy and commitment.

Communication Among All Constituents

In this new age of instant communication, the use of e-mail, newsletters, and the old-fashioned telephone provide a way for principals to inform and be informed by all members of the community. In one newsletter, thanks are given to all who attended the last PTO meeting and participated in the standardized testing discussion. Much of the discourse focuses on the concerns of both parents and administrators as to how to help students. This middle school principal writes:

> The real challenge in teaching is designing curriculum that forces students to think. Thinking is hard work. It offers no quick answers. It only comes naturally to the lucky few. I have often thought that the secret weapon of remarkable students is their interest in thinking about the problem rather that just finding the right answer. Most students were like me, more focused on learning the facts needed for the next test. For us facts are the things that we learn the day before the test and often forget two days after. When I am watching a TV quiz show and I am having a good run, I feel initially smart and then a little foolish. I would trade all my stored memory of baseball statistics and my rapid recall of each of our state capitals for the skills needed to think through a difficult problem. Those are the skills that are worth a million dollars.

His dedication to the education of the students keeps him going. He and other principals use various means of communication to inform the public on how and why programs in the schools help the students acquire the skills they need. We need to redefine the principalship so that these and other gifted principals have adequate time and support to continue to convey ideas and philosophy and remain in the profession. The loss of competent and imaginative leadership will only lead to the loss of decent education for all children—an incalculable cost to American schools.

CHAPTER 5

Negotiating Sustainable Principal Models

Mary Vallone and Lisa Stuart have been close friends and professional colleagues for 12 years. They met in graduate school and, upon completion, procured teaching positions in the same suburban district. They even met their future husbands at the wedding of a mutual friend.

When Mary and Lisa decided that it was time to move into principal positions, they supported each other through the taxing licensure, interview, and induction progression and accepted positions in the same town. It was not shocking to those who knew them that motherhood would also be embarked upon simultaneously.

The issue worrying them the most was how they would balance their time-consuming principalships with the demands of parenthood. With that in mind, they wrote a proposal for their superintendent outlining a job-share arrangement. The unconventional offer was accepted because the superintendent knew that if he did not go along with it, he would likely lose two outstanding practitioners at the same time. A search was begun for a new principal for Mary's school, and Mary and Lisa were appointed co-principals of Lisa's building.

No one was quite sure how it would work, but everyone was willing to try. Their proposal was for a true partnership that split the time and not the responsibilities. Mary was on site Mondays and Tuesdays, whereas Lisa was in the building Thursdays and Fridays. Both were present on Wednesdays. They were challenged by issues of communication, such as parents and students going to one when the other gave an unfavorable response, making certain that everything got done without anything being undone or not done. They used cell phones, e-mail, walkie-talkies, and journals to pass on decisions, priorities, problems, and ideas. In fact, their work was so intertwined that they often combined their names to indicate when they were both working. The office whiteboard would read: "'Mary Lisa' is in today" or "'Mary Lisa' will be back at 2:00 from a meeting in central office."

They are the first to concede that this arrangement is not for everyone. It is not suitable for principals needing full salaries or full control. It also demands a willingness to compromise and collaborate. Obviously, Mary Vallone and Lisa Stuart came to the arrangement with a history of mutual support, respect, and deep friendship. There are also qualities needed by the school system in order to facilitate such an accord.

Mary and Lisa explained that the community must be flexible enough to view each of them as both a separate entity and part of a team. Its members must be able to tolerate a structure that is different from the one they have always known. As for Mary and Lisa, each feels incredibly fortunate to have forged such a unique agreement that honors both their professional and personal lives and that could serve as a model for other principals.

THE CASE FOR NEW MODELS AND STRUCTURES

In many respects, all previous chapters have functioned as an argument for this final chapter on alternative principal models. We have presented a detailed context for understanding the principal shortage and many practical ideas from practitioners on how to negotiate the current expectations of the position. In this chapter we present some models and structures that speak to the many challenges listed by the study's respondents. Since we believe that America's schools need a revolutionary rethinking of how the principal defines and conducts business, we are also proposing a significant alteration of cultural norms, work/life boundaries, and professional expectations.

If we as a country and as a profession are sincere in wanting to improve the nation's schools, then we must be willing to redefine and reconfigure the principal's work so that it supports a more manageable role. We take seriously the testimonies of the principals lamenting tangential tasks, exhausting and all-consuming hours, and outmoded notions about who the principal is and what the principal should look and behave like. We feel that they have made the case for the realignment of tasks to yield educational results for students and professional development for staff.

Patterns emerged from our data confirming that there is no one best way to be a principal or to administer a school. Most of us have known this for a very long time, yet we behave as though an ideal model exists. The study principals reported a disconnect between their work and what everyone perceives their work to be. Although reform efforts have overhauled many of the ways in which we think about the role of the principal, they have rarely provided the resources or will for comprehensive change. Instead, the principal is stuck between the nostalgia of the parents and the utopia of the researchers and reformers.

Neither the nostalgic nor the utopian view changes a job description that includes meager personal lives, professional isolation, and inappropriate expectations from the community. Consequently, we have a new generation of educators who are far less interested in sacrificing their professional integrity and private time to a career that is more focused on accountability for teaching and learning than it is on improving teaching and learning. This is not hard to understand. What is puzzling is that, despite the evidence regarding the shortage, there is so little movement to alter the role. This intransigence must end. We cannot allow a lack of imagination and a misguided allegiance to history and tradition block our ability to provide stewardship for America's schools. We must replace tinkering with best practices and audacity so that Mary Vallone and Lisa Stuart's partnership becomes less of a novelty. Their co-principalship model, and similar permutations, could be one of several alternatives to the current school leadership paradigm.

TWO KINDS OF RESPONSES TO CHANGING THE PRINCIPALSHIP: STRUCTURAL AND CULTURAL

We asked our study participants to reshape the school principalship, at least the parts that challenge their persistence. We asked them to put aside what they have known and think instead of what could be. We analyzed their responses and uncovered the same three tensions that we had seen in the principals' discussions of obstacles and successful coping mechanisms detailed in Chapters 2, 3, and 4.

Their ideas for new principal models addressed the following questions: How can the work be more focused on pedagogy and more attractive to talented educators? How can the job be reconceived to better honor the principal's personal and professional time? How can the principal spend less time at school events and more time on advancing academic achievement?

The principals shared ideas that we felt fell into two categories: structural responses and cultural responses. We defined structural responses as those that include some change in personnel and/or duties, thereby altering the organizational chart and/or job descriptions (e.g., the addition of a business manager). We identified cultural responses as those that modify the principal role by changing building or community norms and/or expectations (e.g., principals can close doors and work undisturbed in their offices).

Linking the Structural and the Cultural

Using our categories, the co-principalship model of Mary Vallone and Lisa Stuart is both a structural and a cultural response to the principalship we have grown to presume. It calls for a job-sharing arrangement that challenges the long-standing one-building/one-principal model and requires that constituencies accept two equally empowered decision makers. The structural change (job sharing) drives a necessary cultural change (community acceptance). In fact, without the cultural change, the structural alteration is doomed. After all, it means nothing to have two people designated as principal but have only one imbued with the authority of the role and the acceptance of the community.

Depending on the need and the available resources, schools can make more or less dramatic changes that encompass structural and/or cultural responses. One of the most significant distinctions between these two categories of response is that structural responses are usually costly, whereas cultural responses are often budget neutral. Paying two principals means double salaries, while changing the community's ideas regarding what the principal does can be a grueling, but free, process.

Putting the Structural and the Cultural in Context

Continuing with the example of Mary and Lisa's co-principalship, there are several issues that challenge principal persistence that are addressed through this creative model. For instance, many of the principals spoke of isolation, of being overwhelmed with work responsibilities, of having little time for reflection, and of a community expectation of omnipresence. By altering the structure so that two people share the burden of the work, the community norms around the principalship necessarily change as well. No one could reasonably expect to see both principals at the school play or PTO (Parent Teacher Organization) meetings when each works half-time, especially when the principals make a point of rarely appearing together at extracurricular events. Needless to say, the cultural shift must occur for the principal as well. If the principal does not lead the way by example, the community will perpetuate the enduring assumptions regarding the principal's constant availability.

BEYOND CO-PRINCIPALSHIP: OTHER FLEXIBLE MODELS THAT ADDRESS THE PRINCIPAL TENSIONS

Certainly, a co-principalship model such as Mary and Lisa's is only one response to the multiple dilemmas articulated in the discussion of the negotiated tensions. There are both other ways of constructing co-principalships and other paradigms altogether. When we asked the study principals what they could imagine as new models that would be responsive to the challenges and contribute to job continuance, they described eight ideas that call for some degree of structural and/or cultural change:

- A co-principalship model in which authority for all tasks is evenly divided, or a model in which lines of responsibility are clearly delineated, such as a principal for instruction and a principal for management. Each principal can be on site every day, or the week can be divided.
- A rotating principalship in which a classroom teacher takes on (and tries on) the principalship for a specified period of time, while the principal returns to the classroom, teaches in higher education, or conducts educational research.
- Role exchanges with university partners or principals from other schools or districts. This would allow the principals to reinvigorate themselves and inform the profession.
- Distributed leadership among many professionals in the building—a model in which some administrative responsibilities are dispersed among members of a leadership team, administrative council, or across the professional staff in general. This is one of the models that could carve out classroom teaching time for the principal, thereby addressing the issue of instructional leadership.
- An expanded role for the assistant principal in which the traditional demarcation of duties is reconfigured to better prepare the assistant for a future principalship and to relieve the current principal's workload.
- Clear divisions of labor between administrative pairs, such as a principal for instruction and a principal for management, a principal and a business manager, or a principal and an administrative clerk. Each of these models has different budgetary ramifications as well as qualification requirements.
- Planned professional development and peer support for the principal sanctioned as a legitimate part of the workweek. These include school visits, conferences, graduate study, community

group meetings, and attendance at principal center events and roundtables.

- A cultural change that permits principals to balance their private and professional lives without associated feelings of guilt. This departure from the usual thinking also argues for fluctuating expectations that temporarily accommodate career stages, a principal's life-cycle needs, or personal priorities.

It is not unexpected that each of the suggestions embodies the notion of moving people in and out of the role, altering the expectations, and/or sharing the work with others. This common approach acknowledges that one person cannot be expected to remain in the position of principal for very long without significant encouragement, ongoing support, and frequent relief from the punishing pace and emotional toll. Embedded is also the belief that we cannot attract people into the principalship as it presently exists.

We all know gifted teachers who refuse to take on these administrative roles because it traditionally means a permanent departure from the classrooms they love. We also know wonderful principals who move into the central office because it is the only available career progression, not their heart's desire. The shortage underscores the need for the profession to recognize these dilemmas and address them through models that nourish and renew our nation's principals.

Models That Promote Professional Development: Rotating Roles and Sanctioning Collegiality

It is noteworthy, yet not surprising, that three of the eight proposed leadership models explicitly promote principal personal nurturance and professional growth. This is consistent with the findings from the foundational study on which this work was based (Boris-Schacter & Merrifield, 2000) and confirms our view that true principal professional development has been neglected. The three models suggested by the principals are rotating principals within the building, role exchanges with educational professionals outside of the building, and professional development built into the principals' workweek.

In each example, cultural shifts by the community and the principal are needed to make the models succeed. Principals have to be willing to relinquish some of their authority and decision making. The school community has to be willing to accept change in leadership or deferred decision making if the principal is out of the building. As a profession, we have to be willing to accept the notions that school leadership can be fluid and that the principal should be supported in ongoing professional development. As is true for teachers, principal professional development could consist of new roles (e.g., returning to the classroom), new places to hold the same role (e.g., swapping principalships with a colleague), and/or engaging in intellectual reflective practice with a focus on improving teaching and learning. Principals can take courses, form study groups, join book clubs, or hold luncheon meetings that are principal-driven.

Principals do get together during the workweek, but these meetings rarely provide a nourishing experience that would combat attrition. Currently, there are too many districtwide principal meetings characterized by "administrative agendas that don't improve instruction." Most of the principals in our study felt that these meetings were a waste of human capital. As one principal explained, "They get us all in a room and out of our buildings, and for what?"

Opportunities for authentic collegiality that are sanctioned by the school districts to take place during working hours could offer one solution to multiple problems. Principals would feel less guilty about leaving the building and doing something for themselves. They would have some support in an otherwise isolated profession, and they would learn new ideas to bring back to their schools. They could actually enjoy their work more.

Similar gains could be garnered by a more extreme approach to professional development: role exchanges. If a principal were interested in trying a central office job, a principalship in a different school, or a clinical professorship at a university, he or she would probably have to resign. Few school districts offer sabbatical opportunities anymore, and even fewer have replaced them with other programs for professional distance, reflection, and growth. Many of the principal respondents felt that they would like to try something else in education and then return to their principalships, refreshed and renewed. This level of flexibility could be just what some educators need to be attracted to the profession or to be convinced to remain in the role.

Clear Divisions of Labor: A Principal for Management and a Principal for Instruction

The vast majority of the study principals suggested a co-principalship as a reasoned reaction to the isolation and overwork of the position. However, few meant the precise arrangement forged by Mary and Lisa. Rather, two people sharing the burden and evenly dividing the work was what most had in mind. Understanding that this is an expensive idea, principals were, nonetheless, not dissuaded from its viability. In fact, of all of the reconceived models imagined by the principals, the most frequent suggestion was a division of labor where there were two full-time principals, specifically one for instruction and one for management.

The rate and passion with which principals cited this notion was completely predictable, given that it spoke directly to one of the core challenges to principal recruitment and retention: the negotiation between instructional leadership and managerial tasks. Although a majority of principals felt that this role separation would aid their persistence, it was stunning that not one principal offered to be the "principal for management." The insinuation is that "head teachers" still think of themselves as educators and thus place instructional leadership at the core of their work. A principal from the Northwest remarked:

> My superintendent thinks we should reorganize and leave the
> principal with the worst jobs. He is suggesting that principals
> do building management and discipline. This is the reverse
> of what I would want and where I think my worth is. I would
> rather be an instructional specialist. Then I could have a dean
> of students who could be in charge of discipline and a full-time
> vice principal for physical plant work.

Based on the principals in our study, we think it is fair to say that most principals would willingly delegate all managerial tasks to a capable and eager partner, even when it means surrendering some power. Perhaps this is a truly viable leadership option that has been overlooked because of cost and tradition. Instead, the idea of principals being more invested in instruction than in management has led some to draw the inaccurate conclusion that schools would be better off with principals who are differently prepared.

Some school districts have responded to the shortage by maintaining the role and appointing principal candidates from the business sector, state departments of education, or the military. These recruits often lack the appropriate background in pedagogy to improve instruction and the grounding in schools to navigate the unique culture. This has, ostensibly, solved one problem and created another. The structural response of two principals or an instructional principal and an administrator is a much more logical course to follow, as evidenced by the remarks of our participating principals.

Altering the School Culture to Accept Change and Flexibility in the Principal's Work

What of the teacher who feels that she must choose between starting a family and becoming an assistant principal, or the principal whose children enter adolescence or whose parent becomes ill and commands more of his time? Currently, most school districts lack a fitting response to career stages and human life-cycle events. This disconnect is salient to understanding the perpetuation of the problems in providing leadership for America's schools.

Mary and Lisa's experience argues that their co-principalship could be a replicable option for principals needing to temporarily accommodate changing work and family circumstances. One such principal is Elaine. Elaine has 12 years of experience operating both an elementary and a middle school, and she urges educators to think creatively and flexibly. She asserts that we remain stuck in old paradigms because we wrongly assume that the community cannot be persuaded to accept new models such as the ones she employed while her children were young:

> When my son was young, I shared the principalship with a colleague. I worked and took the lead three days a week and my co-principal had the lead the other two days. When I was at home with my son, I took care of a lot of paperwork and writing. When my daughter was young, I created a leadership team that allowed me to work 4 days a week and be at home for 1. I have written and spoken about these options and am always surprised by the response by colleagues who insist that "it could never work in my district." I always tell them, "Yes it could. You just have to have the will and the right people involved."

Elaine's experience mirrors ours. We collected much data from principals concerned that their visions of fluid models would not be well received by their districts. A middle school principal told us "I would like to see more of a shared leadership model, but I'm not sure that the culture of a public school would absorb a shared model." Even in a school in the southeastern United States with a co-principalship in place, one of the principals characterized the community's willingness to be open to change as limited:

> I don't know that I could ever appreciably change the position so that I have a better work/life balance. The expectations of the

community will not change. I suppose if I want to affect their thinking, I will have to be willing to be patient and put in the time and the planning.

We wondered about this resistance to change, real or imagined. As Elaine observed, the perception may not be accurate and could be contributing unnecessarily to organizational paralysis, principal resignation, and the national shortage of qualified and willing school leaders. Principals need to be more forthright regarding their needs with their communities, superintendents, and school committees. We suspect that creative ideas for improving the principalship may be more positively received than expected in light of the existing leadership crisis.

There were only a handful of principals in our study who found the life balance they were seeking, seemingly without guilt and still meeting their professional goals. There is one experienced principal, Jed, whose wife works as a teacher and whose two grown daughters live at home, who talked about how he found a way to think about his time differently. In doing so, Jed seems to have altered the school culture so that the community expectations eventually aligned with his priorities and work style. This is, of course, Jed's perspective, but he seems to have molded his principalship to balance his professional and personal priorities:

> Instead of looking at activities, I look at goals each week. I plan
> by week and not by day, and I find flexibility in my schedule.
> I have successfully found more gaps than I initially thought I
> would, and these give me some control over my time. I make
> as few commitments as possible, but I always keep them. I
> left the middle school for the elementary because I felt that [at
> the middle school] I was not only the principal, but also the
> counselor, the custodian, and the hammer and nails. It was
> not fair to my family. I also made the decision to move my job
> closer to my home. A combination of moving to an elementary
> school closer to home and focusing on goals and values rather
> than tasks allowed me to set my schedule so that it was more
> flexible than most principals I know think theirs is. When my
> girls were school age, I never missed any events they were
> in. I would leave school for half an hour and then come back,
> maybe work late. Sometimes I'd take the children home and
> have dinner with my family, then return to school. I actually
> have more flexibility than my wife does as a classroom teacher.
> I often give the advice to administrators that they should seize
> the moment and not feel guilty. I take my daughter out to lunch

sometimes. If I don't have an observation scheduled, I feel I can do it. I would never cancel an evaluation, but otherwise, almost anything can wait. Tasks can be rearranged.

Obviously, with us, the principals were candid and generous. Although few had Jed's successes to share regarding life balance, most acknowledged adaptable models as a desirable response to the demands of the position as well as to the personal circumstances of the principal. For instance, even though Mary and Lisa's co-principalship worked for the school community and for the women while their children were young, it was not necessarily designed to be a permanent arrangement. Like other principals, their work and private lives evolved and their professional demands fluctuated.

Consider a scenario in which Mary is interested in going back to graduate school to pursue a doctorate and a teacher in the building has just earned his principal credential. Potentially, the solution here is to grant Mary a leave of absence to study at the local university and to place the newly licensed teacher in the co-principal role with Lisa. This does require that a classroom teacher be hired, but it also allows for a current teacher to be promoted and mentored within the system. Additionally, there is greater continuity for the school, professional development for Lisa and Mary, and enhanced leadership capacity for the district.

Yet there are few school systems in the United States that would consider such an unorthodox arrangement. Instead, schools have become bastions of old thinking when it comes to educational leadership. Now more than ever it is unacceptable to continue as though nothing has changed politically or socioculturally in our schools. Given the level of principal frustration and a national inability to recruit and retain qualified candidates, it is imperative that we carefully consider the ideas of our principals without being hindered by existing structures and outmoded practices.

Every time we rigidly define the model, we restrict who can fill the role. For instance, if we insist that the principalship be vested in a single individual, then there is no possibility of a shared position. Similarly, if we continue expecting principals to be present at all school functions, then it is difficult to attract candidates committed to both family life and the profession. This mindset has left us with a limited vision and equally limited success.

Instead, we must allow for a variety of possibilities in any given school, over time. Sometimes and in some places, a particular model might suit in perpetuity, but in most settings we should be prepared to think creatively and change course quickly if we want to attract and retain talented educators in leadership positions. We should start actively modifying the principal's working conditions and questioning the field's enduring assumptions if we are to encourage new models and new practitioners.

One Person Can't Do It All: Distributed Leadership Among Many Professionals in the Building

The principals were clear that one person cannot fulfill all the aspects of the job as it is presently conceived. For instance, an elementary principal enrolled in a doctoral program and raising three children under the age of 10 called the usual expectations of the work "ridiculous." She suggested a team approach as a sound way of sharing "the load" and providing much-needed time for reflective practice:

> I think that having one principal in a building is ridiculous. The days of one person carrying the load should be gone. I would love to see co-principals or co-administrators. I would also love to see more handing over of work to people on the staff that are competent and know the building. They know the community, and they really want to work with you. It would be great to create teams of professionals and meet with them. . . . It would be wonderful to have a 2-hour block in the morning where I could work with curriculum teams or psych teams, or building and maintenance people. I would have time to think.

Distributing leadership tasks among staff people in the building was a frequent response to the pressures and workload of the role. The study participants felt that it simply made good sense to distribute the principal work across numerous capable professionals. As was true with the example of Mary's return to graduate school, offering leadership opportunities to teaching staff does the double duty of relieving the principal and providing professional development for those agreeing to take on the tasks. It also supports the notion of sustainable leadership by spreading the work across many players and getting away from the paradigm of the charismatic leader.

Perhaps an even more radical approach would entail not merely a redistribution, but a rethinking. For example, we assume that certain tasks are principal work, but do they have to continue being defined as such? It seems to us, and to many of our respondents, that a willingness to put all the tasks, including teaching, on the table would be prudent at this historical juncture. The most frequent manifestation of this thinking involves the proposal that the role of the assistant principal be significantly expanded. Not only should there be more assistants in more buildings, but the work should change substantially for those in the post.

Rethinking the Assistant Principal Role

When principals are fortunate enough to have an assistant principal, the wisest among them delegates more than cafeteria duty and detention oversight. We already know that educators are less interested in managerial tasks such as these than they are in instructional activities. No doubt, there are many principal aspirants who see the assistant principalship as a necessary step toward their goal, but how many get discouraged along the way? Traditionally, assistant principals remain in the position for 3 to 5 years because they are thought to be apprenticing to the principal. Yet it is usually true that their jobs entail different work from that of the principal, and the apprenticeship analogy breaks down quickly.

Many assistant principals spend little time during the day in the shadows of the principal. Rather, they lead parallel lives in the schoolhouse drama, rarely working closely enough to be accurately portrayed as participating in a mentorship model. The result is the perpetuation of divisions of labor that ill prepare the next generation of school principals, turn many away from continuing in school leadership, and fail to capitalize on the availability of two building-level administrators without classroom-based duties. This underutilization of existing human capital was named by many of the interviewees as one that could be easily rectified.

YOU DON'T KNOW UNTIL YOU TRY

All eight alternative models suggest trade-offs of some kind. Primarily, these trade-offs entail our replacing old assumptions with new ones. Reshaping the principalship so that it offers fluidity of authority and role, as well as ongoing and meaningful professional development, is a big leap. For some the move could be expensive and, as is always true when trying new ideas, would involve a degree of risk. There would be redistribution of power, reeducation of the community, and hard work at communication and collaboration. Implementing any one of these models or combinations of them would not be easy, but ignoring the ideas will surely perpetuate the dissatisfaction of the nation's principals and the continued reluctance from new, talented educators to pursue the role. This is one of many lessons we have learned.

CONCLUSION

Lessons Learned

We began our study in response to numerous newspaper articles and much research data indicating that there was a vast shortage of principals in America's schools. As professors in an educational leadership program at the university, we were also aware of the concerns and fears that our students felt about taking on leadership roles. Their reticence did not bode well for filling the documented vacancies. We pursued a line of inquiry that we hoped would help change the situation.

At the start of our investigation we interviewed successful principals with whom we worked as they mentored graduate students during their administrative practicum. These principals gave us vivid accounts of their work lives. They spoke honestly about impediments to successfully running schools. They also talked about what supported their work. They generously shared experiences and furthered our understanding of what it takes to administer a school in the 21st century. They offered ideas for changing the position so that it could be more manageable, more effective, and more attractive.

We then expanded our pool by contacting principals in other states through more interviews and surveys. The results were striking in their uniformity. Regardless of the school's geographic location, level, size, or socioeconomic status and the principal's race, gender, or tenure, the principals overwhelmingly identified similar barriers to their professional effectiveness and satisfaction:

- Staff evaluation is too time consuming, although central to school improvement.
- Work responsibilities infringe on personal lives.
- Personal life defines professional boundaries.
- Roles, responsibilities, and number of hours spent working increase yearly.
- Gender bias endures in the principalship.

- Life circumstance and professional experience frame the concept of balance.
- The community's vision of the principal is bound by tradition, preventing flexible models from being developed and implemented.
- Too much time is spent on administrative tasks and paperwork, especially since the passage of the No Child Left Behind Act of 2001.
- Too little time is allocated to instructional leadership and professional development.

All of the principals we interviewed and surveyed cared deeply about their work. Some, however, actively addressed the obstacles that blocked their goals of professional accomplishment and personal satisfaction. They found ways to examine how they used time, set priorities, and acted on them. The principals reflected on their work and asked questions that assessed the quality of their leadership, such as the following:

- Am I spending too much time maintaining the status quo?
- Am I spending my time implementing the academic agenda?
- Am I engaging in some activities simply because there is no one else to do them?
- Am I engaging in activities because they have always been the responsibility of the principal or because I think they have educational importance?
- Are there activities that, if not done, would allow more time for focused instruction or professional development?

These questions led to a further set of inquiries regarding the relevance of certain administrative tasks to the educational mission:

- Am I the only one who can do the task? If not, what might be stopping me from delegating the work?
- Would I get more done and/or more done that I think is important if I had help?
- What would constitute authentic help?
- Are there new resources that need to be acquired or existing resources that could be reallocated?

PRINCIPAL STRATEGIES

The principals identified strategies for managing competing demands on their time and explained how they aligned those demands with their personal views of effective leadership. Those with staying power described coping mechanisms that were artfully and purposefully created. Organizing their day in detail allowed them to get work done while preventing their professional responsibilities from encroaching unduly on their personal lives. Broadly defined, the mechanisms involve workload sharing, emotional sharing, personal nurturance, and the application of customized rules to the balance of time and work. The principals in the study coped with the inordinate workload by doing the following:

- Scheduling and structuring classroom visits
- Actively involving school personnel in teacher evaluations
- Setting aside time for personal nurturance and professional reflection
- Increasing teacher participation in tasks traditionally assigned to the principal or assistant principal role
- Deliberately allotting time slots for work to be completed at home
- Protecting time for personal pursuits, thereby enhancing knowledge and sensitivity that invariably returns to the school in the form of new skills and new outlooks
- Working with parents to review community expectations that restrict the principal's role
- Sharing emotional and task-related burdens of leadership with personal partners and professional colleagues, including forming principal groups

LEADERSHIP COUNTS

Even those who successfully developed and used coping strategies felt that revamping the principal's role and reeducating the public could make a significant difference with respect to both recruitment and retention. Most principals were ready to suggest alternative leadership models, indicating that they had spent time thinking about what changes were needed. They recommended a bold departure from the traditional leadership role and the long-held assumptions regarding what matters most. They argued that the time had come for policymakers to seriously rethink the job responsibilities and support the implementation of flexible and fluid leadership models such as the following:

- A co-principalship/job-sharing model
- A rotating principalship within the building and among buildings
- Higher education and K–12 partnership in which roles are exchanged
- Distributed/collaborative leadership, such as a leadership team or administrative council
- Clear divisions of labor among multiple administrators (e.g., a principal for instruction and a principal for management, a principal and a school manager)
- An upgraded and reconceived assistant principal role
- Structured and sanctioned professional development and peer support for the principal
- The creation of a cultural shift that facilitates a balance between the private and professional lives of principals

We are not suggesting that these ideas or others could be implemented easily or quickly. We know that school culture does not change overnight. What we are arguing is that we should respond to the observations, struggles, and ideas shared by the principals in this study if we want to address the shortage of qualified and willing principal candidates. We never questioned whether leadership counted; we just never knew how hard it was for America's principals to lead.

WHAT IS NECESSARY TO CHANGE THE PRESENT UNSATISFACTORY SITUATION?

First, we need to recognize current limitations—an inefficient system of governance that burdens the principal with bureaucratic tasks that infringe on his or her time to deal with more pressing educational needs. Next, we need to acknowledge that we are facing an urgent and, in many areas of the country, a critical challenge—the loss of qualified leaders who are too frustrated to be willing to continue in the role. The difference between a seasoned teacher's salary and that of the principal is not substantial enough to attract teachers to apply for the position. Many universities have created innovative programs to train candidates, but a gap still exists between theoretical and practical enthusiasm for the position. Efforts to recruit "fresh" leadership from the ranks of retired military and corporate personnel have failed to solve the problem of dwindling instructional leaders.

Principals said that they entered the position primarily to help students and to assist teachers. In the present school system, this goal is very difficult to accomplish. In rethinking the principalship, we need to implement changes that allow school leaders to provide the service they deem integral to effectively run a school.

The principals we interviewed and surveyed have excellent suggestions to improve the role, make it more efficient, and serve their students better. We learned from this investigation that in order to attract and retain motivated principals, we must provide them with support, give them the freedom to make meaningful decisions, and trust them to work toward offering the best education for all students. We need to disturb acquired educational habits and expectations so as to force a reconceptualization of school leadership roles in a way that unshackles our most creative educators from the constraints of bureaucratic regulations, however well intentioned.

The study principals did not ask for a total dismissal of current educational systems. Their innovations were based on experience and reflection, centered on the needs of students and teachers, and not predicated on huge financial investments. Their voices deserve to be heard, and their ideas merit implementation. There is no question in our minds that the time has come to renegotiate the principalship. The benefits will exceed the risks, and one could hardly ask for a sounder reason to heed the call for change.

APPENDIX A

Research Methodology

The research for the book was based on a pilot study conducted from 1998 to 1999 by Sheryl Boris-Schacter and Susan Merrifield (Boris-Schacter & Merrifield, 2000). The impetus for that work was also the national shortage of qualified principals, but the focus was different. In the pilot, Boris-Schacter and Merrifield approached the problem of the principal shortage from the perspective of investigating what is rewarding in the job. We already knew that long hours, multiple constituencies, low community status, and legislated systemic change made the principalship an emotionally draining undertaking. Consequently, we suspected that those educational leaders who remained in administrative positions must have found ways of sustaining themselves. To find out what enabled principals to survive in a role that was becoming increasingly less attractive, we interviewed 19 experienced Massachusetts practitioners about what they thought constituted meaningful professional development.

We gained some valuable insights into what these principals do that might be contributing to their persistence. One of the findings was that the principals found ways of integrating their personal passions into their professional lives. What piqued our interest even more, however, was a consistent response to an unasked question. Eight of the 19 principals talked about the enormous challenge they faced in balancing their work and personal obligations, even though we asked nothing about it. Given that our questions focused on professional development, the arena of balance suggested additional research that could address the looming principal shortage.

Based upon this finding, we (Langer and Boris-Schacter) constructed a new interview guide (see Appendix C) and spoke to 10 additional principals. What we uncovered was that balancing home and work responsibilities was an issue that resonated with every respondent. We took the findings from this combined sample of 29 elementary and middle school Massachusetts principals and presented them at a national conference.

The room we were assigned had a capacity of 125. Before the session even began, there was standing room only. We opened our talk by asking how many attendees were principals; every hand shot up, save two. We had exactly the audience we needed to discern whether the line we were pursuing was as meaningful as we suspected. The attendees confirmed that the findings we presented mirrored their experiences, and they suggested that further investigation could inform the field and affect the shortage. The conference principals' ideas were invaluable and their encouragement for us to press on was unequivocal.

They told us that we needed to engage in a study that included a wider range of participants. Specifically, they suggested that we gather data from high school principals and practitioners from a larger geographic area. They urged us to build on the diversity of our original sample of 29 that included men and women; White principals and principals of color; novice and veteran principals; principals from rural America, from the suburbs, and from urban centers. We agreed and we complied.

Between 1999 and 2004, we conducted more Massachusetts interviews and spoke with principals from four additional states—52 principals altogether. The new principals we included were purposefully selected using similar criteria to those of the original 29. They were all known to the interviewers, had strong reputations in the education community, and held positive attitudes about the profession and about their work. In the course of the interviews, some of the participants shared pertinent documents. These were primarily principal-generated newsletters and internal school district memoranda. We used some of the data from those documents to illuminate aspects of the principals' work or to better understand the local thinking about the principal's role.

To increase the sample size without the expense of face-to-face interviews, we added surveys to our design (see Appendix D). These were disseminated electronically to all principals in a school district. Sometimes districts were chosen because of prior personal relationships and other times they were selected for their size, reputation, location, or varied student population. Over the course of the data collection, we actively sought participation from school districts and from individuals who met our study parameters. For example, if we found that we lacked a district from the Pacific region or from rural America, we pursued its inclusion. Similarly, we collected and analyzed individual demographic data so that we could feel confident that a range of voices and experiences were represented. Combining the interview states and the survey states, we solicited school districts from all geographic regions of the United States: Northeast, South, Great Lakes, Central and Mountain, Southwestern, and Pacific.

Regardless of our systematic approach to gaining wide participation and representation, we understand that a sample with a range of age, race, gender, number of years of experience, and presence or absence of children at home says nothing about the quality of the practitioner. We gave consideration to the quality for the interviewees, but we could not control any of the variables for the survey respondents. As is always true with survey research, we can only guess that those who participated had something to say that may or may not be the same as those who did not return the survey. Ultimately, we analyzed data from 52 interviews and 151 surveys (see Appendix B for respondent characteristics).

The interview data were recorded using fieldnotes and, in addition to Boris-Schacter and Langer, who conducted the vast majority of the interviews, there were four other research assistants. Two of these assistants were doctoral students, one was a school principal holding a doctoral degree, and one was a doctoral-level school superintendent.

The data analysis was based on a coding system designed by Boris-Schacter and Langer after exchanging fieldnotes, coding them separately, and comparing them for interrater reliability. The codes we ultimately agreed on grew organically from the data and were conceptualized in the context of the theoretical frameworks offered by Robert Kegan and Michael Lipsky (see Chapter 1 for a full discussion). The way we made sense of the codes became the big ideas for the book: negotiation on several levels and the three identified principal tensions. We applied these same codes to the qualitative data returned in response to the survey instrument and to the unsolicited documents provided by some of the interviewed principals.

A research assistant, under our direction, inputted the demographic data from the surveys into StatView. She reviewed data regarding the conditions that we felt could potentially affect principal balance. They were gender, race, school level, number of working hours, and whether there were children living with the principal. She examined the interaction among the variables to determine whether any group or groups reported a disproportionate burden or ease. For instance, she looked at questions such as, "Are women principals reporting more children at home?" or "Are male principals of color reporting logging in more hours at the workplace?" Of course there were individual exceptions, but she found no significant differences across groups. In fact, what was so compelling with respect to the interview data was equally compelling regarding the survey data. There was an overwhelming consistency about the ways in which the principalship was being experienced by these 203 principals.

The methodology veered from conventional qualitative procedure in that we did not strive to triangulate with multiple sources. In fact, all of the interview and survey data were self-reported and the documents were self-selected. Some would view this as an inherent design weakness.

However, we think that it was appropriate to the research question. It seemed to us that if we were interested in knowing how principals feel about what challenges their persistence and job satisfaction, it only made sense to ask the principals directly.

To attempt triangulation through gathering data from other sources for the purpose of refuting and/or corroborating principals' opinions of their own work seemed beside the point and repetitious of others' errors. Instead, we chose to gather data that would, together, paint a portrait of how these principals viewed their work obstacles, supports, and vision by interviewing and surveying principals from all regions of the country and with a variety of personal and professional characteristics.

APPENDIX B

Respondent Demographics

	Interviews, 1998–2004	Surveys, 2000–2004
Gender		
Male	26	54
Female	26	97
Race		
White	41	107
Non-White	11	44
Grade level		
Elementary	33	90
Middle school	24	33
High school	5	28
Geographic location		
California		74
Florida		22
Illinois	3	2
Iowa		8
Kentucky		8
Maryland	1	
Massachusetts	27	16
Montana		10
New Hampshire		2
North Dakota		9
South Carolina	6	
Washington	5	
	(*N* = 52)	(*N* = 151)

APPENDIX C

Interview Instrument

1. Relevant demographic information (personal):

   Gender

   Race

   Number of years as a principal

   At what level is your current principalship—elementary, middle school, or high school?

   Identify the people in your life for whom you have major responsibility, either in caretaking and/or in partnership (if children are included here, please indicate their ages).

2. Relevant demographic information (regarding the school district):

   Is your school district best described as rural, suburban, or urban?

   Would you categorize the majority of family incomes in your school as being lower, middle, or upper socioeconomic level?

3. How many hours a week do you spend working?

4. How many hours a week do you spend thinking about work-related matters?

5. How do you set priorities when there are equally compelling obligations to work and to home?

6. What have been the major challenges to realizing your professional priorities?

7. What strategies have you used to meet these challenges?

8. If you could start from scratch and redesign the principalship so that it is a more attractive career choice, what would it look like?

9. If you made those changes, would other changes necessarily follow, such as changes to the school culture or the organizational structure?

10. Is there anything else that I should have asked and didn't?

APPENDIX D

Survey Instrument

We are sending this survey to you as part of research that we as Lesley University professors of educational leadership are conducting on the ways in which school principals balance work responsibilities with personal lives. This e-mail has been sent, with permission from the superintendent, to every principal in your district. Its analysis, along with that of interview data and document review, will become a book that addresses the issue of the national shortage of school leaders and will suggest alternative models for a more manageable principalship. The voices of working principals from across the country must inform the policymaking. Therefore, we hope that you will spend 10 minutes filling out and returning this survey electronically. The identity of individual respondents and their respective responses will only be known to the researchers and their assistants. Please feel free to get in touch with us if questions arise. We are very grateful for your participation.

1. Relevant demographic information:

    Gender

    Race

    Number of years as a principal

    At what level is your current principalship—elementary, middle school, or high school?

    Identify the people in your life for whom you have major responsibility, either in caretaking and/or in partnership (if children are included here, please indicate their ages).

2. Is your school district best described as rural, suburban, or urban?

3. Would you categorize the majority of family incomes in your school as being lower, middle, or upper socioeconomic level?

4. How many hours a week do you spend working?

5. How many hours a week do you spend thinking about work-related matters?

6. How do you set priorities when there are equally compelling obligations to work and to home?

7. What have been the major challenges to realizing your professional priorities?

8. What strategies have you used to meet these challenges?

9. If you could start from scratch and redesign the principalship so that it is a more attractive career choice, what would it look like?

References

Archer, J. (2004). Tackling an impossible job. *Education Week, 14*(3), S3.

Blackman, M. C., & Fenwick, L. T. (2000). The principalship: Looking for leaders in a time of change. *Education Week, 19*(29), 46, 68.

Bolman, L., & Deal, T. (1997). *Reframing organizations: Artistry, choice, and leadership.* San Francisco: Wiley.

Boris-Schacter, S. (2001). Classroom contradictions. *Education Week, 20*(25), 42, 47.

Boris-Schacter, S., & Langer, S. (2000, March). *Reconstructing the principalship in the new millennium.* Paper presented at the annual meeting of the Association for Supervision and Curriculum Development, New Orleans.

Boris-Schacter, S., & Langer, S. (2002). Caught between nostalgia and utopia: The plight of the modern principal. *Education Week, 21*(21), 34, 36.

Boris-Schacter, S., & Merrifield, S. (2000). Why particularly good principals don't quit. *Journal of School Leadership, 10*(1), 84–98.

Bradley, A. (1992). New study laments lack of change in Chicago classrooms. *Education Week, 11*(27), 1, 19.

Callahan, R. E. (1962). *Education and the cult of efficiency.* Chicago: University of Chicago.

Christensen, G. (1992, April). *The changing role of the administrator in an accelerated school.* Paper presented at the annual meeting of the American Educational Research Association, San Francisco.

Cotton, K. (2003). *Principals and student achievement: What the research says.* Alexandria, VA: Association for Supervision and Curriculum Development.

Cusick, P. (2003). Why teachers won't trade the classroom for the office. *Education Week, 12*(36), 34, 44.

Davidson, D., & Gooden, J. (2001). Are we preparing beginning principals for the special education challenges they will encounter? *Educational Research Service Spectrum, 19,* 42–49.

Deal, T., & Peterson, K. (1999). *Shaping school culture.* San Francisco: Jossey-Bass.

Driscoll, D. (2004). Massachusetts' schools chief offers "feel-bad" education cure. *Education Week, 24*(9), 43.

Education Writers Association. (2002). *Searching for a superhero: Can principals do it all?* Washington, DC: Author.

Educational Research Service. (1998). *Is there a shortage of qualified candidates for openings in the principalship? An exploratory study.* Study done for the National Association of Elementary School Principals and the National Association of Secondary School Principals. Arlington, VA: Author.

Educational Research Service. (2000). *The principal, keystone of a high-achieving school: Attracting and keeping the leaders we need.* Arlington, VA: Author.

Esparo, L. (2000). *Leadership under pressure: The administrator crisis in our public schools.* Providence, RI: Education Alliance at Brown University in collaboration with the Connecticut Association of Boards of Education.

Evans, R. (1996). *The human side of school change.* San Francisco: Jossey-Bass.

Fenwick, L. (2000). *The principal advisor* (Vols. 1, 3). Cambridge, MA: The Principals' Center.

Fisher, R., & Ury, W. (1983). *Getting to yes: Negotiating agreement without giving in.* New York: Penguin.

Friedan, B. (1997). *Beyond gender: The new politics of work and family.* (B. O'Farrell, Ed.) Washington, DC: Woodrow Wilson Center Press.

Gilman, D. A., & Lanman-Givens, B. (2001). Where have all the principals gone? *Educational Leadership, 58*(8), 72–74.

Goodman, E., & O'Brien, P. (2000). *I know just what you mean: The power of friendship in women's lives.* New York: Simon & Schuster.

Goodson, I., & Hargreaves, A. (2003). *Teaching in the knowledge society: Education in the age of insecurity.* Berkshire, UK: Open University Press.

Hallinger, P., & Heck, R. (1998). Exploring the principal's contribution to school effectiveness: 1980–1995. *School Effectiveness and School Improvement, 9*(2), 157–191.

Hurley, J. C. (2001). The principalship: Less may be more. *Education Week, 20*(37), 1.

Institute for Educational Leadership. (2000). *Leadership for student learning: Reinventing the principalship* (School Leadership for the 21st Century Initiative: A Report of the Task Force on the Principalship). Washington, DC: Author.

Johnson, S. M. (1996). *Leading to change.* San Francisco: Jossey-Bass.

Kannapel, P., & Clements, S. (2005). High-performing, high-poverty schools: Lessons learned from research. Retrieved March 15, 2005 from http://prichardcommittee.org/

Kegan, R. (1982). *The evolving self: Problem and process in human development.* Cambridge, MA: Harvard University Press.

Keller, B. (1998). Principals' shoes are hard to fill, study finds. *Education Week, 17*(27), 3.

Kozol, J. (1991). *Savage inequalities: Children in America's schools.* New York: Crown.

Kozol, J. (2005). *The shame of the nation: The restoration of apartheid schooling in America.* New York: Crown.

Leithwood, K., Janzi, D., & Fernandez, A. (1994). Transformational leadership and teachers' commitment to change. In J. Murphy & K. Seashore Louis (Eds.), *Reshaping the principalship: Insights from transformational reform efforts* (pp. 77–98). Thousand Oaks, CA: Corwin.

Levine, J. A., & Pittinsky, T. L. (1997). *Working fathers: New strategies for balancing work and family.* Reading, MA: Addison-Wesley.

Lieberman, A. (1995). Practices that support teacher development: Transforming conceptions of professional learning. *Phi Delta Kappan, 76*(8), 591–596.

Lipsky, M. (1981). *Street-level bureaucracy: Dilemmas of the individual in public service.* New York: Russell Sage Foundation.

Lovely, S. (2004). *Staffing the principalship: Finding, coaching, and mentoring school leaders*. Alexandria, VA: Association for Supervision and Curriculum Development.

Mishra, R. (2003, February 5). Repetition makes best surgeons. *Boston Globe*, p. A1.

Monroe, L. (1997). *Nothing's impossible: Leadership lessons from inside and outside the classroom*. New York: Times Books.

Murphy, J., & Seashore Louis, K. (Eds.). (1994). *Reshaping the principalship: Insights from transformational reform efforts*. Thousand Oaks, CA: Corwin.

Ostrow, E. (2003). An academic life out of sync. *Chronicle of Higher Education*, p. C5.

Pappano, L. (2003, December 21). In many classrooms, a principal lesson. *Boston Globe*, p. B11.

Pfeffer, J. (1992). *Managing with power: Politics and influence in organizations*. Cambridge, MA: Harvard Business School Press.

Rimer, S. (2002, December 15). Philadelphia school's woes defeat veteran principal. *New York Times*, p. 141.

Rosenholtz, S. (1985). Effective schools: Interpreting the evidence. *American Journal of Education, 93*(3), 352–388.

Roza, M. (2003). *A matter of definition: Is there truly a shortage of school principals?* Paper presented at the annual meeting of the American Educational Research Association, Chicago.

Rutter, M., Maughan, B., Mortimore, P., & Ouston, J. (1979). *Fifteen thousand hours: Secondary schools and their effects on children*. Cambridge, MA: Harvard University Press.

Sarason, S. B. (1982). *The culture of the school and the problem of change*. Boston: Allyn & Bacon.

Smulyan, L. (2000). *Balancing acts: Women principals at work*. Albany: State University of New York Press.

Steinberg, J. (2000, September 3). Nation's schools struggling to find enough principals. *New York Times*, pp. 1, 18.

Winerip, M. (2003). On front lines, casualties. Retrieved November 17, 2003, from http://nytimes.com/2003/09/24/education/24EDUC.html

Yerkes, D. M., & Guaglianone, C. L. (1998). Where have all the high school administrators gone? *Educational Leadership, 28*(2), 10–14.

Zuckerman, D. (1999). *On common ground: Prominent women talk about work and family*. Washington, DC: Institute for Women's Policy Research.

Index

Accountability
  and expectations/definitions of
    leadership balance, 56, 60, 61, 62
  and instructional leadership-
    management balance, 21, 27, 30
  and models for principalship, 73
  and understanding the principal
    shortage, 8, 9, 10, 15
Archer, J., 13
Assistant principals, 75, 82–83, 86, 87
Authority
  and expectations/definitions of
    leadership balance, 54, 56, 58, 65, 68
  and instructional leadership-
    management balance, 20, 27
  and models for principalship, 74, 75,
    76, 83
  and personal-professional balance, 39
  and understanding the principal
    shortage, 9
Autonomy, 68

Balance
  expectations and personal definitions of
    effective leadership, 53–70, 86
  factors influencing concept of, 84
  instructional leadership-management,
    17–33
  and lessons learned about principalship,
    84
  and national study, 13–16
  personal life-work, 13–14, 34–52, 86
  and tensions of principals, 2–3
  and understanding the principal
    shortage, 7
Blackman, M. C., 10, 11, 12
Bolman, Lee, 28, 69
Boris-Schacter, S., 8, 10, 12, 48, 62, 76
Bradley, A., 10
Business managers, 21

Callahan, R. E., 11

Central office, 26, 27, 31, 53, 54–56, 61, 67,
    76. *See also* Districts
Change
  need for openness to, 79, 88
  principals as agents for, 63
  resistance to, 79–80
  See also Reform, educational
Christensen, G., 10
Chronicle of Higher Education, 19
Classrooms
  transitioning to office from, 15–16
  visiting, 18–19, 26, 31, 34, 41, 86
Clements, S., 13
Co-principalships, 71–72, 73–75, 77–78, 79,
    81, 82, 87
Coalitions, 64–66
Collaboration, 53, 57–58, 62, 63, 72, 83, 87
Collegiality, 65, 76–77
Communication, 64, 65, 68, 69–70, 71, 83
Community
  balancing personal definitions of
    effective leadership and expectations
    of, 53–70, 86
  defining the, 54
  and instructional leadership-
    management balance, 20
  and lessons learned about principalship,
    85, 86
  and models for principalship, 72, 74, 76,
    79, 80, 83
  and outside demands on principals, 1
  and personal-professional balance, 40,
    43, 45, 49
  reeducation of, 59, 66, 83
  and standards of practice for reshaping
    principalships, 6
  and understanding the principal
    shortage, 11.
  See also Expectations; Parents; Unions,
    teacher
Compatibility, 26–28
Compensation. *See* Salaries

About the Authors

Sheryl Boris-Schacter, a former reading teacher, special educator, secondary English teacher, and school administrator, is a professor and the director of Educational Leadership at Lesley University. She is the editor of *The Changing Relationship Between the Principal and the Superintendent: Shifting Roles in an Era of Educational Reform* and the author or co-author of articles on professional development, policy, and the school principalship. She has an Ed.D. from the Harvard Graduate School of Education and resides in Newton, Massachusetts, with her husband, Bill, her son, Blake, and her daughter, Tess.

Sondra Langer, formerly an early childhood and elementary school teacher and supervisor of student teachers, is presently an associate professor at Lesley University and the director of the Early Childhood Program in the Graduate School of Education. Prior to her tenure at Lesley, she was an adjunct professor at Tufts University, Boston University, Northeastern University, and Simmons College in Massachusetts. She has co-authored articles on educational leadership and has presented at many workshops on the school principalship and on early childhood curriculum and issues. She holds a B.S. in education from City College of New York and a M.A. in educational administration from Simmons College. She lives in Newton, Massachusetts, with her husband, Lawrence.